W9-BON-365

16/89

A Season for Wilderness

A Season for Wilderness

THE JOURNAL OF A SUMMER
IN CANOE COUNTRY

Michael Furtman

NorthWord
PRESS, INC
Box 1360, Minocqua, WI 54548

Designed by Moonlit Ink, Madison, Wisconsin

Illustrations by Susan Robinson

NorthWord Press, Inc.
Box 1360
Minocqua, WI 54548

For a Free Catalog describing NorthWord's line of nature books
and gifts, call 1-800-336-5666

ISBN 1-55971-005-5

◆ DEDICATION ◆

To Mary Jo,
who in life, as on all our wilderness canoe trips,
goes before me with beauty and enthusiasm;
and to my friend Gypsy, whom I miss.

✦ ACKNOWLEDGEMENTS ✦

I would like to extend my thanks to those dedicated people of the U.S. Forest Service who made our season in the wilderness possible. Special thanks go to Barb Soderberg in the Duluth office of the Superior National Forest and the Rangers of the Kawishiwi District; Jerry Jussila, Jim Hinds, Chip Elkins, Gil Knight and Pete Weckman who shared with us not only their expertise but friendship.

I am grateful as well to Carol Stolcis who took the time to straighten out some of the kinks in my contorted sentences.

I am also fortunate to have been able to work with Susan Robinson whose powerful and sensitive artwork so wonderfully captures our adventure and graces this volume.

This book would not have been possible without the quiet confidence expressed in me by NorthWord Press and Tom and Pat Klein. I am much obliged to them for the opportunity to tell our story.

Finally, there would have been no season in the wilderness for us without the foresight and hard work of those groups and individuals who have struggled so long to preserve the canoe country and wilderness in general. The battle yet rages on. We are all in their debt.

·CONTENTS·

Introduction

JUNE

JULY

CONTENTS

AUGUST

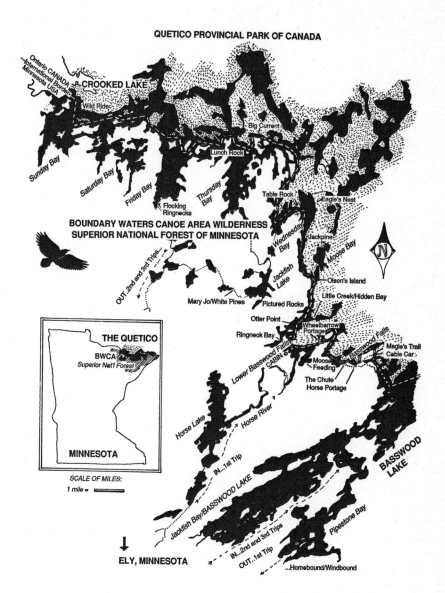

QUETICO PROVINCIAL PARK OF CANADA

CROOKED LAKE

Ontario CANADA
International Border
Minnesota USA

Wild Rice

Big Current

Lunch Rock

Sunday Bay

Saturday Bay

Friday Bay

Thursday Bay

Flocking Ringnecks

Table Rock

Eagle's Nest

BOUNDARY WATERS CANOE AREA WILDERNESS
SUPERIOR NATIONAL FOREST OF MINNESOTA

Wednesday Bay

Jackpine

Moose Bay

OUT...2nd and 3rd Trips

Jackfish Lake

Olson's Island

Mary Jo/White Pines

Pictured Rocks

Little Creek/Hidden Bay

Otter Point

Ringneck Bay

Wheelbarrow Portage

Magie's Trail
Cable Car

Basswood Falls

Lower Basswood Falls

CABIN

Moose Feeding

THE QUETICO

BWCA
Superior Nat'l Forest

The Chute
Horse Portage

MINNESOTA

Horse Lake

Horse River

BASSWOOD LAKE

SCALE OF MILES:
1 mile ■

IN...1st Trip

Jackfish Bay/BASSWOOD LAKE

Pipestone Bay

ELY, MINNESOTA

IN...2nd and 3rd Trips

OUT..1st Trip

...Homebound/Windbound

xiii

◆ FOREWORD ◆

In reading *A Season for Wilderness*, I'm reminded that the Boundary Waters Canoe Area is meant for all seasons and for all time, past and future as well as present.

Let me examine first the matter of history. I once read a report by a paleobotanist, J. E. Potzger, of Butler University, after his extensive boring deeply into muds of bogs and lakes and digging into foot-deep sphagnum moss. "To the imaginative analyst," he wrote, "the whole observation is an ever-changing scene of great throbbing life activities." Why so? Dr. Potzger elaborates on the analyst's revelations:

"He reads into the tiny pollen grains great forests. He hears the purring west wind in furry boughs. He pictures snow and ice, cloudy and sunny days, rushing streams of spring freshets, death crashes of great tree giants weakened by centuries of combat, germination of seeds and new forests. As he counts he wonders how many deer, wolves, bear, spruce hens and varying types of scurrying animal life were associated with these changing forests."

We all ought to travel slowly, linger and contemplate the ancient story of particular parts of our little planet. Paleobotany is a specific science, but Dr. Potzger has shown that imagination can prove as helpful as the microscope or computer. Imagination works wonders even without the tools and training of science. It works best, I daresay, free of all restraints, when the observer conceives life as timeless, eternal, and space as limitless, leading only to space beyond.

That must be how the Indians viewed the Boundary Waters, the Sioux who came first, followed by the Chippewa, or Ojibway. They were as much a part of the forest as trees, water and wildlife. Their whole existence revolved around the powerful intertwined forces of nature and religion. Because they believed they were descended from forest animals, their clan names and totemic emblems represented wildlife—the bear, loon, heron, moose, eagle and catfish.

Those early people understood stars, sun, moon, and seasons because they were in close contact with the elements. They knew nothing of convenience, but they recognized that the animals and plants could manage on their own with humans, while humans, for all our brain power, cannot make it without the benefit of plants and animals. That viewpoint was superseded, of course, with the arrival of European culture. The explorers, trappers, traders, lumberjacks, miners and settlers allowed little time to identify themselves as small players in the grand tableau of history. I picture the scene of a century or so ago, when roads were cleared, sawmills and stamp mills erected and mining towns arose in the wilderness. It was something of a free-for-all.

The border-lakes country, as we know it now, might all have been gone, long gone. The wilderness of today is no accident of natural history, though it may have started as such, but the result of unending battles and strenuous efforts of particular individuals endowed with high ideals and bold ideas. I like to slow down a while, as did Michael Furtman, during his special summer in the Boundary Waters, to think of the men and women who selflessly safeguarded the treasure in the heart of the continent when it was tough to do so; they inspire kind thoughts about humankind and hope for it.

I envy Michael the summer he experienced in the Boundary Waters with his wife and dog. Still, I recall the Christmas that I spent in this wonderful country. It was in 1986. My son came up from Dallas and we headquartered at the YMCA lodge on Burntside Lake, spending days skiing over the frozen lakes and the hills, examining animal tracks, and lavishing in the gift of sheer quiet. At night we repaired to the sauna, heated by firewood; then, pretending we were fearless Scandinavians, plunged into a small pool carved out of the frozen lake, after which we sat, each wearing only a towel, to absorb the wonder of the wintry night skies.

FOREWORD

In other countries to visit someplace like the Boundary Waters would be sought as a privilege. In our country we accept it as a right. Michael Furtman reminds his reader that with right comes responsibility.

It isn't really difficult to exercise responsibility. Actually it brings a stronger sense of belonging. It bonds the present with the past and provides a gift to the future. Anyone who reads this book will enjoy his own canoe more, and slow down the paddle to better observe and deepen perception of one of the superlative preserves on earth. May it always be so.

Michael Frome

◆ INTRODUCTION ◆

Auspicious undertakings often begin unremarkably. So too was the beginning of our adventure which stemmed from a small news release in our newspaper one Sunday in March, 1986. In two paragraphs the release stated that the U.S. Forest Service (USFS) was looking for summer volunteers to work in the Superior National Forest and the Boundary Waters Canoe Area Wilderness (BWCAW), the latter lying within the former and both located in northeast Minnesota.

To someone who had roamed this country for many years, and who as a youth had read many adventure stories about wilderness travel and forest rangers, the thought of being able to be one for a summer, long after another career choice had been made, was irresistible. After discussing it with my wife, Mary Jo and making an application to the Forest Service, events progressed swiftly.

The application alone was exciting. There, under the caption "position" read "wilderness ranger." Wilderness Ranger! My too fertile imagination turned loose, I could already conjure visions of my wife and I bronze skinned and strong, fighting fires, aiding injured campers, clear eyed and resolute standing on some rock point in the canoe country, gazing over indigo waters and surveying our assigned territory. Perhaps even our black Labrador retriever, Gypsy, would get into the act and sniff out a lost child who had wandered from camp, a child we would find alone and crying in the tangled forest and whom we would carry back to the distraught parents to their everlasting thanks. They would praise us, offer us gifts and promises, all of which we would gently refuse. "No thanks, ma'am. Just doing our job," we'd reply and paddle off into the sunset. Filled with anticipation, we awaited a reply to our application.

Upon the acceptance of our application there was a rapid exchange of letters and phone calls with the Forest Service offices in Ely and in Duluth, our home town. It was decided that we would live and work out of the Crooked Lake cabin, located near the Lower Falls of the Basswood River. Canada would be just across the water. We would be responsible for campsite and portage maintenance from the top of the river at Basswood Lake, west across Crooked Lake to Curtain Falls. We would also range south to Wagosh Lake and then east through the small lake country to Jackfish Lake.

I could hardly contain myself when thanking Barb Soderberg of the Duluth Forest Service office and Jim Hinds and Jerry Jussila of the Kawishiwi Ranger District in Ely for the opportunity. Under the guidance of these rangers and others, we and perhaps forty other volunteers were given a two day crash training course. The others, fresh faced young men and women of college age were in this for their own reasons, many looking for the experience the volunteer positions would give them toward possibly related careers. It was obvious that Mary Jo and I were the oldest volunteers on hand, both of us in our early thirties, she a Mathematics teacher and I a writer.

In two compact days we learned the basics of trail and campsite maintenance, how to dig and install a latrine, how to deal with the public, check permits and handle violators. We also learned, much to our delight, that we would be participating in some basic wildlife surveys, keeping count of the whitetail deer we saw and observing the eagle and osprey nest in our territory to mark the success of their nesting efforts. We even learned to howl like wolves, to howl so that they will respond. If we managed to contact a wolf pack that information would be useful to the biologists in locating the wolves' summer range.

Mary Jo and I would be in the wilderness for nearly three months, paddling out only twice to resupply. The Forest Service would pay us each $4.00 per day to help with food costs and would supply what equipment we would need. We opted to use much of our own equipment, including our beloved wood and canvas canoe. Though we would be based out of the cabin, our territory was too large to cover in a day and we would be camping out part of the time. We requisitioned a tent, pots and pans, stoves and whatever else we might need from the Forest Service.

Here was an opportunity for us to really get close to the canoe country, to see it in all its moods, to put our finger on the pulse of the wilderness. This land had seen many changes since the days when it was inhabited by the Ojibway and was highway to the Voyageur. It had been logged and developed, resorts having sprung up even in the interior. It had been embroiled in fierce political battles between those who wished to develop its resources further and those who wanted to retain its wildness. Now, on each side of the international border, Ontario's Quetico Provincial Park to the north and the BWCAW to the south, over a thousand lakes and two million acres are set aside by the respective governments as a mostly non-motorized wilderness. After becoming a protected wilderness, the resorts within the BWCAW were purchased and razed and the canoe country began to settle down.

In our position we would be able to observe not only the wilderness, which in essence has changed little, but how its management was working and how it was being treated by its current users. Aside from those more practical observations, we were looking forward to steeping ourselves in the rhythms of this land, of being able to have the time to absorb its sights and sounds and to listen to its voice.

If we are open to it, the wilderness will speak to us in many ways. Sometimes it will whisper to us, its peaceful voice stirring things deep within us; emotions, fears and hopes that we have in common with our ancestors who lived so much closer to the land than we. In its most illuminating voice, a voice of calmness and introspection, it opens to us a world of thought, thoughts not given the time to mature in our everyday harried lives. Darker and more twisting than any forest of the natural world, the wilderness of our mind has clear paths delved through it by the light of nature.

Wilderness can scream at us too, though this scream is a far cry from the raucous noise of the city. It is the scream of an eagle or the dying wail of some prey. It is the howl of a storm through the trees or of the wolves along a ridge. It is the roar of the surf as we struggle to paddle our canoe to shelter, the scream of excitement, challenge and adventure, the part that awakens us to the sheer joy of living.

All of these things, from the digging of latrines to the sublimities of nature, would be ours for awhile. For one summer, in a world where most spend but a week or two, we would know no other life. The outside world would nearly cease to exist.

This book is the story of our summer. I make no boasts of it being a grand adventure, of it being of great importance. But to all who know and love the wilderness, especially those who have been captivated by the magic of the Quetico-Superior canoe country, I hope to make our experience yours, to share with you some insights gained from that summer. I hope that you can grasp some of our excitement, feel our frustrations and sense the canoe country's majesty. If I write much about our, and particularly my, thoughts and impressions, it is because, as Thoreau said, "I should not talk so much about myself if there were anybody else whom I knew as well." We all are, to paraphrase him, limited by the narrowness of our experience.

Arrived in Ely, Kawishiwi District Office, USFS, at 8:15 a.m. Picked up the needed equipment and were shuttled to Mudro Lake landing.

Left Mudro Lake at 10:00 a.m. Arrived at Crooked Lake cabin at 7:30 p.m. after "walking" the majority of the Horse River. The heavily loaded canoe and low water level made the river difficult traveling. Even so, it was a beautiful day for canoeing with deep blue sky, white clouds and virtually no wind.

Retrieved stashed gear hung in white pine a block southwest of the cabin. Encountered a black bear while lowering the pack.

◆ NEAR THE FALLS ◆

Basswood River's Lower Falls were lit by the golden glow of sunset. The Canadian fork flowed amber in the waning light as we portaged the last load of equipment past the roaring cataract. It was 7:30 and nearing the end of a very long day, our first day in the canoe country as wilderness rangers.

As soon as we were within sight and sound of the falls we breathed a sigh of relief. Having been this way only two weeks earlier in order to check out the Forest Service cabin that would be our home for the summer, we knew that we were drawing near. With the one last portage around the falls, we only had to haul our month's supplies to the cabin and retrieve the goods stashed in the woods from our last trip before we could collapse.

We had the right to collapse. This trip was far removed from our normal lightweight canoe trip. Leaving Mudro Lake we had the accumulated piles of gear, tools and food we would need to do our job, supplies that would have to last until the end of the first week in July when we would paddle to town to restock. I estimated that our load, less the canoe, was near four hundred pounds.

Included in that load were two food packs, two gear packs, one small but heavy pack containing cameras and fishing tackle, a heavy two-way Forest Service radio, a Coleman lantern and two burner stove, two gallons of white gas, a pack for our dog stuffed with twenty pounds of dog chow and a canvas gear duffel containing fifty plastic trash bags, an axe, cross-cut saw, bow saw, broom, claw hammer, pliers and miscellaneous nails, screws, hinges and hasps. Somewhere in the canoe we managed to stuff a large box of oakum and a cumbersome soil auger.

It was all we could do to get so much gear into our seventeen foot canoe. With Mary Jo in the bow and myself in the stern, the gear every inch between us, Gypsy had to squeeze into the small space at Mary Jo's feet.

Still, we left Ely with a great deal of anticipation in our new adventure. Nearly three months in the Boundary Waters Canoe Area Wilderness of northern Minnesota seemed like a dream come true. Though the three of us have ventured on many canoe trips up to a month in length, this challenge of the summer we knew would be something entirely different. We would not just be paddling for the sheer pleasure of it, we would be living and working in this beautiful country. As is the nature of beginnings, we had no clear idea of what direction this summer would take.

Though our load was heavy we made good time through Mudro, Sandpit and Murphy Lakes, enjoying our work, even the double and triple portages. By the time we reached Horse Lake and the headwaters of the Horse River we were ready for lunch. Not anxious to unload the canoe in order to go ashore, we ate while we drifted about on Horse's clear waters. The day was fine and warm with scarcely a breeze to impede our progress. Lazy white clouds lounged in the west, drifting slowly across the brilliant blue sky. I could feel the warmth of the early summer sun on my neck, seeking out the pale flesh that soon would turn brown. Buoyed up by our lunch we looked anxiously to the run down the Horse River, feeling sure that our day's work must be nearly half done.

The Horse River flows north out of the lake through a rocky narrows. Two weeks earlier we had managed to sneak the canoe through the ragged teeth of the first rock garden by hugging the east bank. As we neared the first little rapids this time we quickly became aware of how much change had taken place since last we had passed. Gone was the deep, narrow chute through which we had plunged. Now the entire entrance to the river was guarded by row upon row of protruding boulders through which no path wide or deep enough to pass a canoe could be seen. Our choices were also limited by the fact our craft was so heavily laden. Routes that might have been deep enough to float a lighter load were simply too shallow for us. The thought of portaging the heavy cargo down the rubble strewn bank was not the least bit inviting.

In the end there was nothing to do but try to walk the loaded canoe past the boulders. With the three of us out of the boat it floated a bit higher but still required much lifting and tugging, often with us standing thigh deep in the cold water, to get it over the many obstacles. Every time the canoe's canvas skin slid over a rock, bits of red paint floated downstream and I cursed silently and often not so silently. Eventually we managed to get to deeper water and piling in soaking wet, we floated to the next rapids.

The one really good rapids on the Horse might be runable in some water conditions but today there was no choice but to portage around it. This rapids takes a sharp easterly turn around a rock escarpment and then shoots through a straight, but boulder-filled, chasm. Two weeks earlier we were able to easily line the canoe both down and up this rapids, the latter on the way home in late May when an enormous hatch of black flies was occurring. Black flies hatch in moving water and the whole of this rapids was abuzz with them then, a moving cloud three feet thick hovering over the water for a hundred yards. By the time we had lined to the top of the rapids, the red canoe was nearly solid black with flies. Mary Jo and I were equally covered with the dastardly little vampires and Gypsy was long gone, hiding in the cedars back in the woods where she knew she would find some relief. Fortunately for us on this much slower trip, the insects were not nearly so numerous. We made the portage without much difficulty.

There are three portages you can count on taking on the Horse River at any time of the year, but this day found that we were bound to make more than that. The heavy load and low water made walking through many rapids necessary, a lesson painfully learned when one attempt resulted in a glancing blow from a hidden, canoe-eating rock, a sickening cracking sound evidence that we had done some damage to a cedar plank in rib. Resigned to the conditions, we would pile out every time the water grew shallow, feeling by the end of the day we had walked most of the river instead of paddling it.

Still, the fine weather and the wandering river made the long day enjoyable. Many turtles were taking advantage of the sun by warming themselves on rocks and logs along the shores. At one point we saw three turtles in a line on one log, each a little larger than the next. With the largest turtle on the upswept, narrow tip of the tapered log and the smallest turtle near the thick end disappearing into the water, it was a confusing display of depth perception.

The lower part of the Horse before the final portage is slow and meandering and a spot that would seem perfect for moose, though we saw none this day. Alerted by our duck dog's quivering, we followed her stare to the shore to see two mallards standing atop a nearly submerged log, the male with his iridescent green head sparkling in the sun, his mate almost invisible next to him. This, to me, was a sign of spring and though it was early June now, we were not so distant from the snows and ice that had lately engulfed this far northern country. The mallards had paired off to mate and it would be many weeks before we would see any ducklings.

It somehow seemed fitting that we would start our adventure at the beginning of the summer. We would have a chance to enjoy the canoe country throughout an entire season, watching the progression of the year. Though we would leave our duties in late August, I knew too that autumn comes early here. We would feel the first cool nights and the mountain maples and birch trees would show early hints of color before we left.

We completed the portage around Lower Basswood Falls, taking the Canadian side because of the fine, sandy upstream landing that made beaching the canoe simpler and because the Canadian portage is lovely as it winds along the edge of the falls through a beautiful

stand of Norway and white pines. It was a heady feeling to be there, as tired as we were, smelling the resin-scented air and listening to the song of the river, knowing that this ancient path of the Indian and Voyageur would be our road to work on many days.

The Crooked Lake cabin, as the Forest Service building at Lower Basswood Falls is known, lies near the tip of the point that comprises the American side of the falls. It is not readily visible from the water and the first real sign that any structure is there, unless you are very observant, is the old log boathouse down on the water's edge. This building is the same size and vintage as the cabin and sits near the end of a blind bay immediately to the south of the falls, perhaps thirty rods from the cabin. It is nestled in a low spot between two rock promontories. The rock to the right of the boathouse, as you view it from the water, is shrouded in a dark forest of spruce and balsam. To the left, the huge round rock slope is covered with caribou moss, blueberry bushes and pine.

Though there was supposed to be a dock near the boathouse, we could see no sign of it. As low as the Horse River had been, the Basswood River, of which this portion of Crooked Lake is but an extension for a few more miles, was seemingly in flood. While we debated where to land, the dropping sun lit the scene before us and as morning and evening light so often do, heightened the hues of the myriad colors. The boathouse was awash in soft light, the faded color of the old logs now a warm, mahogany brown. The light struck a lone birch behind the boathouse, its white spire brilliant as it gave the illusion of growing straight through the peak of the building's roof. All around, the woods were a new green, green as it appears after a rain.

It was an inviting scene. I pointed the bow toward the grassy bank just to the left of the boathouse doors. Though her back was to me I smiled at my wife and dug the paddle into the water for the last few strokes.

"Let's go, Hon. We're almost home."

Home. What a beautiful sound. And what a beautiful place to call home.

6

It was the day to make this old, neglected log cabin our home.

Swept and washed cabin floors, cleaned cupboards, tables, aired bedding, built a door jamb from scrap lumber and put a hasp and hook and eye lock on back (kitchen) door. I also fixed the hasp on the boathouse door and buried some old food we found in the cabin. While Mary Jo continued cleaning I began filling cracks in the walls and floors with oakum. Talked to campers in campsite below cabin.

Celebrated our first day here with a ration of brandy and a fine dinner of venison chops cooked to perfection.

♦ ON OUR WAY ♦

I suppose there are less pleasant ways to wake up than to the friendly voice of Jerry Jussila over the two-way radio. Jerry was our immediate supervisor, Forest Service Ranger and our link to the outside world. Still, I was startled to awaken to his voice crackling over the airwaves and not the buzz of our little travel alarm which I had set for an hour before this prearranged, and daily, check-in call.

The exhausting day before, when we had arrived at our home for the summer, had put both Mary Jo and I in such a deep sleep that the little clock was never even heard. I rolled over in my sleeping bag to make a stab for the radio microphone.

"Crooked Lake, Crooked Lake, this is Ely, " Jussila droned in that professional Forest Service voice they all adopt on the radio. The zipper jammed on my sleeping bag and without my glasses, or a free hand to find them, I was having a difficult time getting free.

"Crooked Lake, Crooked Lake, this is Ely."

My hand shot out and snared the microphone. I didn't want to let them know we'd slept in so I put on my best wide awake voice.

"Ely, this is Crooked Lake. Good morning Jerry," I chirped.

"Good morning, Mike. Glad to see you made it. Was everything OK at the cabin?"

I quickly ascertained that the radio, for official business only with no chit-chat, was not made for lengthy explanations so I condensed yesterday's experiences.

"Fine, except we were met by a few hundred mice and a bear. Nothing we couldn't handle though," I replied.

We had been warned about the cabin's true owners, the mice, and were supplied with mousetraps. Jim Hinds, another wilderness Ranger at Ely, had joked about the size of the trap line we'd have to run and had alluded to the record number of mice trapped during a summer, which ran around two hundred. Judging by the amount of mouse droppings we'd already seen, and the amount of scurrying we'd heard after shutting down the Coleman lanterns before drifting off to sleep, we'd undoubtedly be in contention for usurping the record.

"Good," Jerry said with a chuckle in his voice and then moved on to check-in with other crews in the field, ending with the daily weather forecast.

While Jerry conversed with others, I listened and got dressed. The 7 a.m. radio call was a daily ritual, we'd been told, during which crews would receive instructions, relay messages or ask questions. No doubt we were not the first ones to use it as an alarm clock either. While most people who go to the canoe country prefer not to have any contact with the harried outside world, and on a normal canoe trip neither would we, the thought of having the radio, a means of seeking help or advice, was very comforting as we faced our new duties.

As I listened to Jerry contact the other crews I glanced over at Mary Jo. She was still groggy in her sleeping bag so I shuffled into the kitchen and put a pot of coffee on the stove.

Gypsy also looked a bit tired, curled up on an old blanket we found in the cabin. Besides the long day portaging in, during which she carried her own dog food in pannier style dog packs, she had been up half the night with mice running around her floor level bed. At one point, just as I was falling asleep, I heard her get up and dash across the room after a mouse, only to crash into the wood stove in the dark, unfamiliar cabin.

The mice weren't the only wild creatures we'd encountered since we reached the cabin. I hadn't been kidding Jerry about the bear.

Two weeks before we moved into the cabin for the summer, Mary Jo, Gypsy and I paddled in for a short reconnaissance trip. After spending a weekend at the little cabin we decided that rather than haul out all of our gear, we would stash some of it there, making our next trip in easier. Items such as sleeping bags, foam pads, tent, tarps and the like I put into a Duluth pack and not wanting to leave them in the unlocked cabin, I hiked a quarter mile back into the forest and hung them in a large white pine, food pack style.

So it was that yesterday upon our arrival, tired though we were, I had to retrieve our gear, lest we have to sleep without our comfortable bags. Except for those, the remainder of the items could have just as well waited for morning.

By the time I had headed back into the dark forest the sun was already behind the hills. I followed the shoreline for a short distance to the south to the end of the bay, found a hog back ridge heading into the woods and used it as a guide to the big white pine. The foliage was much thicker now than it had been two weeks earlier and I must confess that I got turned around once or twice. I would spot the spire of a tall pine, bull my way up to it only to find it was the wrong tree. On my third attempt I succeeded in locating the right pine.

Modern man may have lost many of the senses of his primitive ancestors, at least on a conscious level. Our receptors may still pick up the data but our brain, lacking the proper program, fails to register a response. There is one sense, however, that all of us can claim and that is the feeling of being watched. No doubt in more dangerous times this sense was vital.

As I began to untie the rope I hesitated uneasily. I was being watched. There was no doubt in my mind. By whom or what, I had no idea, nor certainly where. I started to scan the area slowly and out of the growing shadows loomed a blackness that was darker than its surroundings. Now that I had something to focus on I quickly identified the creature. It was a bear.

I have read all the research that says that black bears are very rarely dangerous. Mostly black bears are shy but they can be big, opportunistic rascals, raiding campsites and scaring campers, showing just enough aggression to obtain food. Pests, yes; dangerous, rarely. That much I knew.

Face to face at twenty yards with a very, very large black bear in a forest that was quickly growing dark, I realized that everything I had ever read seemed ridiculously trite. Darkness is the dominion of fear. Big animals, ones with lots of teeth and sharp claws, mix readily with that darkness to create an air of absolute electricity. Which is why my hair was standing on end.

It occurred to me then that this bear, seeing me lowering a pack from the tree, would no doubt assume that it contained food. Hanging your food in a tree is a common way of protecting it from marauding black bears in the canoe country and because some campers are less adept at this technique than others, many bears have learned that this situation can lead to easy pickings. I had no doubt that this bear had dined on freeze dried lasagna in the past. It was almost dark. I needed to make a decision. I was tired and irritable and wanted that pack at least as much as the bear did.

"Hey bear!" I screamed, "Get outa here."

The bear stood on its hind legs to better see over the meager brush that separated us. Doing so, he seemed to grow ten times in size. I picked up a big stick.

"Gowan, get outa here!" I yelled again.

This time the bear took off as if a bee had stung its nose. It crashed downhill at tremendous speed, going over and through the brush rather than around it. Then it stopped. It stopped in the darkness between me and the route back to the cabin, completely out of sight in a heavy tangle of spruce and alder. The dark forest suddenly grew very still. Without the noise I could only wonder whether the bear had simply stopped and was watching and waiting or had slipped quietly away. The silence was ominous.

It was dark now. I quickly lowered the pack, unwrapped it from the waterproof tarp, stowed the tarp in the pack and shouldered the load. And then, with a tingle in my spine and a flutter in my heart I lifted my voice in song and headed back to the cabin.

I have a lousy voice. But I can sing loudly. Loud enough, I hoped, to let the bear know exactly where I was and where I was going. This was no time to meet nose to nose in the dark timber.

I sang something, to the tune of the "Yellow Rose of Texas" (I don't know why that song came to mind) that went, "Look out bear I'm coming, you must let me through; I'm heading to the cabin, but you're not welcome to." Silly perhaps, but the bear did let me through. I kept singing until I saw the light of the Coleman lantern in the cabin window.

Mary Jo had been nervously waiting, especially after it grew dark. She knows that I'm comfortable in the woods, but she realized after I had left that she had no idea in which direction I had gone. She began to worry what she would do if I did not return. Fortunately for both of us, she never had to make that decision nor did I have to spend a night in a tree.

We both knew that this incident would not likely be the last one involving a bear that we would experience that summer. But the first encounter was behind us now.

It was a new day. A pot of coffee later and we were both ready to start work. I took Gypsy for a short walk around the cabin to the two nearby campsites.

The Crooked Lake Cabin sits on a peninsula running northeast to the Lower Basswood Falls. The cabin faces principally north and sits on high ground perhaps fifty yards from the water. Since the USFS wants to make the log cabin as inobtrusive as possible to the BWCAW's visitors, they have allowed the surrounding growth, mostly balsam and aspen, to grow up and shield the cabin from view. It would take an observant eye to spot the structure, even while paddling nearby.

The boathouse, on the other hand, sits squarely on the water's edge near the south end of the bay. While it is visible to those paddling offshore, most paddlers never enter the bay, their attention attracted by the magnificent cataract and their search for a portage. No doubt thousands have passed within a few hundred yards of both structures without spotting them.

Sharing the peninsula with the cabin are two campsites. To the north of the cabin, very near the base of the falls, sits the first site. The second, at the top of the falls, is east of the building. Neither is visible from the cabin.

Both campsites are ancient and undoubtedly were used by not only the Voyageurs, Ojibway and Sioux but by even more ancient visitors. It is a logical place to camp for anyone traveling this way by water, either after making the numerous portages around the rapids of the Basswood River as one passed down, or a fitting resting spot for those who have paddled the length of winding Crooked Lake.

The upper campsite was empty. It is a pretty site, hidden from view from the river by a rock knob, the tent pads on the flats set back from the river under the spreading limbs of huge pines. Rust needles from the pines cover the area and make it look clean, soft and inviting. Behind the camp is a ridge of granite, covered in a luxurious bed of pale green caribou moss. Delicate bunchberry plants, veined, egg shaped leaves cradling tiny white flowers as if they were a fair gift to be presented on only the best platter, grew amongst the club moss and asters. While Gypsy climbed down to the water's edge for a drink, I sat listening to the roar of the falls.

I have always been impressed by the scale and grandeur of the canoe country. It is a hard and bony land and were it not for the linking waterways the area would scarcely be penetrable. Unlike the grand vistas of mountain country, the canoe country allows you only glimpses of its magnitude. Almost furtively it leads you on, down narrow lakes or winding rivers, opening itself only gradually to the explorer. One can sit atop a mountain and contemplate an entire region; in the canoe country one sits only on small lichen covered knobs, surveying intimate scenes. But it is exactly this shyness that is the canoe country's charm and one must probe it slowly and over long years before knowing many of its secrets, before sensing its grandeur.

This river, scoured out by the flow of the last glaciers, has been a highway for uncounted years.

Journals of Voyageurs frequently mention these falls and the churning Basswood River. More than just a few careless courier du bois

paid his dues to the Misshepezhieu, Ojibway spirit of waves and currents, along this route, no doubt adding to its notoriety among these tireless canoemen. The rapids, tempting to run to avoid portaging heavy loads, have probably eaten canoes, goods and human lives since the first canoe traveled this way.

A large blue heron fished in a pool halfway down the falls, standing in a backwater up to its knobby knees, frozen nearly in midstride by my arrival, its topknot drooping. The giant grey bird launched itself into the morning mist as I stumbled down the trail along the river and beat its way slowly downstream toward Crooked Lake.

As you approach the lower campsite there is a high knob of granite thrusting north from the base of the falls that provides for an impressive view. The falls of the American side churn noisily below. Across from this rock point is the island that is also on the U.S. side of the border and the portage trail that drops steeply from its crest where, in 1800, Alexander Henry the Younger described it as "a portage of about 100 paces over a rock." He obviously had not much of the poet in his soul. The Canadian falls to north of the island shoots forcefully from the rocky chasm through which it sweeps, split first by a big glacial erratic at its crest and then careening in a white froth around a bend, all currents meet suddenly in a foamy and swirling cauldron of black water before turning north toward confusing Crooked Lake.

There is great power in that triple falls, power that you can know with all senses. Its thunder is both felt and heard and when one nears the falls' mists, you can feel them lying wet upon your skin, taste their slightly fishy flavor. It is not a place one would forget quickly.

The second campsite was occupied. I could hear quiet voices over the sound of the falls, smell the wood smoke of their breakfast fire. Gazing down the expanse of the river, past the little islands, tall pines and the distant bluff where the pictographs share ancient magic with all who pass, I was awed by the beauty. This was our territory, our responsibility. The importance of that charge was beginning to sink in.

I tucked in my shirt tails, ran my fingers through my unruly hair and checked my Forest Service name tag before I climbed down from the bluff to introduce myself to the campers. It would be my first official contact and I wanted to look presentable. I clapped Gypsy to my side and sauntered into the camp. We were on our way.

Took a cruise to Wednesday Bay to start our eagle survey but were caught in a thunderstorm and forced to sit it out on shore. Talked to three groups of canoeists and gave them weather reports. Discussed wilderness ethics with one youth group that we witnessed dumping soapy water into the lake.

Upon returning to the cabin we continued to tighten up the cracks.

✦ OTTERS ✦

What a joy! On our way back from Wednesday Bay, just south of the pictographs where the river widens into the first large bay, we paddled up on five otters. Hugging the west shore to stay out of the strong wind, we were upon them suddenly as we rounded a point and caught them in the midst of their frivolity.

Otters are always great fun and these were no exception. My only wish is that they would have stayed to perform longer. Once they spotted us, three stood high in the water, up like periscopes, and hissed at us. Perhaps it was the presence of Gypsy in the bow of the canoe that alarmed them more than usual, for after the dog and otters exchanged sniffs and snorts, they swam swiftly down the shore.

It is hard to not like otters. I know of no other animal in the north that seems to have so much fun. If I were to have to become an animal, the otter would be a logical choice. They are so carefree.

It seems as though they have an easy life, although, not being an otter, I might be presuming much. With food plentiful, no real predatory threats, and equipped to handle the elements as they are, it appears that they have the time to frolic and play games.

I have followed their winter tracks to find the places where they slide and have many times come to hills, usually on the edges of creeks or lakes, where the snow has been parted with furrow after furrow of otter belly marks. Can you imagine the sheer fun of being able to, at any time the whim comes to you, flop down on your belly and slide down a hill? Without getting snow down your neck? On Quetico Lake, in the far northwest of the canoe country, there is a shore of high cliffs along the lake's north arm. On these rocks is what is known as the Quetico Gallery, an impressive display of Indian pictographs. Mary Jo, Gypsy and I were paddling along one part of the gallery on a hot, summer day, looking for what has become one of our favorite pictograph displays, the portrait of the woodland caribou. I suppose I feel drawn to this likeness because the caribou no longer roams the canoe country, their habitat changed when lumbermen removed the area's pine. Because I would have liked to have seen the canoe country before the logging, before the people, before the borders and rules and regulations, I have become enamored with the caribou. They left as the others came. Perhaps, if they return, some of the oldest magic will come with them.

As we paddled along the base of the cliff we were entertained by a lone otter, swimming in Quetico's clear waters. No doubt he was fishing. All along this shore it is not unusual to be able to look down into the depths and see many shadowy forms of fish. Annoyed that we were disturbing his fishing, he started to search the cliff face for some crevice in which to hide. At this point we picked up our paddles and began to move on, leaving him peeking out from between two rocks, thinking he was hidden.

What happened next had never happened to us before and will likely never happen again. I caught a blur of movement out of the corner of my eye from high up on the cliff face and turned quickly towards it. Dropping from a height of twenty or more feet came the hurling bodies of two full grown otters, plummeting through the air in a dive to the lake. Either they were not aware of us before their leap, or misjudged our position, or even were simply being mischievous. Whatever their intent, they missed landing in our canoe by only feet. Mary Jo and Gypsy, forward in the canoe, could not see the dive and were startled by the loud splashes so near. I sat with paddle across my knee in disbelief at what I had just seen. It was quite a few moments before we could paddle on and the time was spent watching the Otter Air Force swim away.

As playful as they are they are also curious. Cirrus Lake, north of Quetico Lake, is divided into three tiers, connected by channels. As we camped on a point in the upper most tier we were startled one night to have three otters visit. I awoke to the movement of Gypsy in our tent and was sure that there must be a bear in camp, the normal reaction of any camper faced with night time noises. I put my hand on Gypsy's shoulder and instead of feeling her hackles up, and the throaty rumbling growl she uses to warn bears to keep away, I felt her trembling in excitement. I could see her silhouette against the moonlit tent and her ears were up in the manner of all curious dogs.

Gypsy moved closer to the tent wall and began to sniff through the fabric. Immediately came a similar snuffling from outside followed by the sound of moving animals all around us. As the animals pressed noses through the thin layer of nylon, my own curiosity grew.

Cautiously unzipping the tent door, just enough to peek my head outside, I flipped on the flashlight, apprehensive I might go nose to nose with a bear. My fear soon turned to a chuckle when I saw a sleek otter poking around the other end of the tent, peering cautiously back at me. Suddenly two others appeared and they all huddled together in the light, bobbing up and down and bristling their whiskers, a pyramid of otters. As long as the light was on them they stayed but when I finally turned it off they turned and sinuously made for the lake, swimming off into the moon dappled waters.

What brought them to our tent, one can only speculate. My guess is that in the moonlight they saw its silver dome in a spot where nothing had been the night before. Since this campsite is used only rarely, sometimes unoccupied for years, they were interested in finding out who had moved into their neighborhood. I doubt they thought we'd be good neighbors.

I hoped though that these otters today, so near to our cabin, would not mind us sharing this spot with them. I hoped that if we were good neighbors, the otters would stop by to entertain us from time to time.

These were neighbors we could live with; bright, playful and harmless. Any place that was fit for otters, I thought, was the kind of place I'd like to be.

We continued on to the cabin, the constant drone of the falls growing louder as we neared. There is a big island just west of the falls and as we neared it a mature bald eagle powerfully swept from the boathouse bay, so low to the water the massive wings nearly left dimples. When it reached the Canadian shore it climbed quickly and landed in a big norway pine, tottering for a second before securing its grip.

A few more strokes and we were passing the last campsite before the island. There is a narrow, shallow channel between the campsite and the island that we use as a shortcut to the boathouse. As we passed the camp we watched one of the occupants dump a pan of soapy water into the lake. I quickly changed courses to talk to this man and as we approached he nonchalantly hid a bar of soap.

As we paddled away I silently apologized to our neighbors, the otters and eagles. I hoped they wouldn't hold the actions of others of my species against me and would stop by for a visit again. We would do our best not to foul the neighborhood and maybe, through our efforts, help others to do the same. After all, that's what being good neighbors is all about.

Went upstream to Horse Portage today to inspect and clean all unoccupied campsites.

Walked entire U.S. side of the Basswood River from site #5 to cable car where I found an old blaze trail and walked it out to portage.

Found and dismantled two old illegal camps. Thoroughly cleaned three campsites by sweeping debris from bedrock, scrubbing latrines, cleaning out firegrates and policing area.

With the heat and hard work we became quite pooped out. Not too pooped, though, for me and Gypsy to take the canoe out near dusk for a bit of fishing. The bass weren't biting but I did catch two dandy pike on surface plugs.

◆ MAGIE'S TRAIL ◆

This ranger work (or as Mary Jo calls it: wilderness maids) is hard.

Not being used to this level of physical exercise, and the fact that it was very hot today, may account for our fatigue. I believe all the tools we lug around with us has something to do with it as well. A list of the items we must travel with is as follows:

one cruising axe	one bow saw
one point shovel	two hard hats
one broom	gloves
one latrine brush	one hammer
one canvas bucket	miscellaneous nails, screws, bolts
one pair brush snips	one two-way radio (which holds
one cross-cut saw	twenty D size batteries).

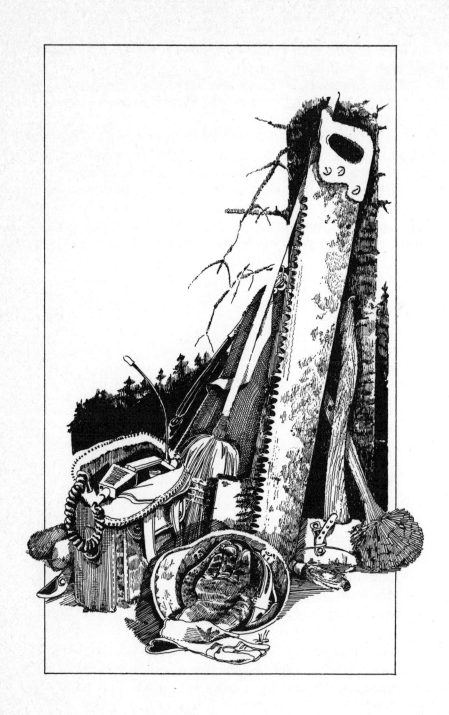

Add to that other important items such as lunch, camera gear, rain gear and a first aid kit and our daily excursions take on the proportions of an expedition. All the tools are hauled in a military-type duffel, handles extending from the top. This is carried from a shoulder strap and hangs down with the shafts pointing forward. Mary Jo calls it "the golf clubs." Everything else fits in a day pack or a Duluth pack.

Mary Jo carries her golf clubs, the life jackets and paddles while I portage the canoe and pack. We make good time on portages.

Today we explored the Horse Portage for the first time and found the area to be stunning. The river courses serpentine through the granite slash in the hills, alternating between dangerous rapids and powerful slicks. The voyageurs used to break this long portage up into two shorter ones, navigating some of the more reasonable white-water between major rapids. The volume of inexperienced canoeists using this area now are wise to use the longer portage and leave the risk of river running to those more skilled or foolish.

We inspected all six campsites along this part of the river. All but two of them are reached by trails branching from the portage, the other two situated on either side of the irregular point jutting into Canada and reached by water.

I found the maid work tiresome today and asked Mary Jo if she cared if I explored the river a bit. My excuse was that I would walk the bank and look for user sites (USFS jargon for illegal campsites as opposed to the legal, designated sites) and inspect the camps further up the river. Mary Jo approved of my plan for she is an agreeable woman who understands my need to explore. I left her sweeping the wood chip, twist tie and cigarette butt debris from the bedrock in site #5. We would meet later for lunch.

Gypsy, my constant companion, and I wandered up the winding river.

The river here varies in width, from a mere fifty yards up to one hundred. With the unbroken blue of the sky today it ran blue-black and with power. There is little doubt what would be the outcome if a canoe turned sideways in these rapids.

The Canadian shore to the north is generally higher and more rugged than the U.S. side although there are very steep sections to both. Where the rock tips gradually into the swirling waters it changes color from ash grey, to green-black and finally to blue-black. The green tint is from the algae that clings tenaciously to the shore, anchored against lapping waters. Treacherous when stepped on, this growth has spilled many a traveler who, climbing from his canoe, plants a foot on what is believed to be abrasive rock. In the winter, when all plant life here dies or grows torpid, it releases its grip on the rock, finally scraped away by the clashing ices of spring. It is this brief time of grinding ice that harkens back to the era of glaciers, repeating their scouring process on a miniature scale. It is also what gives all great rivers of the north that clean, almost barren look for few plants can abide such grinding.

I once witnessed such an ice-out on the Knife River of Lake Superior's north shore. I can only imagine that it must be much the same here on the Basswood. As I watched the water flowing serenely through the clinging shelf ice of the Knife one spring I became aware of a rumbling to the north. Within moments the water level dropped as somewhere upstream of me the ice formed a dam holding back the flow and then, more quickly than one would ever believe, a rampart of ice swept the river bed carrying with it trees, boulders and stumps. Huge slabs of clear ice, as big as cars, were shoved up high onto the banks to await their sunny demise. Within moments the wall had passed and the river was again peaceful.

Although it was hot today, in the valley of the river I felt the coolness of moving water. Drawing from the chill of the deep underbelly of sprawling 14,000 acre Basswood Lake, the river seemed to moderate the heat of the air.

In places blueberry bushes grew in profusion, some squat to the rock, others knee-high reaching for sun. Wood irises, tangerine in color, splashed the hunter green of the forest floor. Junipers clung to slopes and jack pines probed deeply into cracks in the bedrock, searching for secure moorings in this valley of wind and water.

It was utterly beautiful and utterly wild.

We came to a place of open rock, a point that dared constrict the current. A circle of blackened rocks sat back on a knob and I wandered over to the fire ring. It is illegal now that the crowds have come to the canoe country to build a fire on the American side anywhere but in the iron grates provided by the Forest Service, a necessary measure because of those who would build fires in places unwise. This ring, however illegal, was in a safe spot, a place I myself would have chosen had I camped on such a slab in the Quetico where the location of your fire is still your choice. On clean rock and near the water so that one would need only walk a few paces to fill a pail, it was a campsite of your dreams. Nonetheless, I moved to remove it since leaving such things only encouraged others to build fires outside of the grates.

The ring was old. Lichens were growing on some of the rocks and the charcoal debris had washed away from the interior of the ring. I hesitated before bending over to pick up the rocks. How old was this ring? Could it have sat here the one hundred and fifty years since the last voyageur braved these rapids? Was this an artifact or litter?

I squatted to roll the first rock, the headstone of the ring and stopped only when I heard a high pitched scream. Lifting the rock as gently as I could I uncovered a small black bat that had been hiding in the crevice between this rock and the next. Exposed to the blinding day, it made hissing sounds much larger than its body, spreading leatheren wings flat against the stone.

I lowered the rock gently and walked away. Whether artifact or litter, this rock ring was now someone's home.

Upstream both Gypsy and I waded into the water for a drink and to cool down. I also needed to rinse the charcoal stains from my hands, rubbed there from breaking up two much more recent, and messier, illegal camps we had found a short distance away. I could feel the power of this river, a swift grip pulling steadily, even though I was only boot top deep. Gypsy leaned backward from her drink, lapping at the current, biting bubbles as they swept by, sensing even with her limited capabilities the danger of the current.

The hillside on the U.S. side grew steep and I cut back into the forest and up the slope. Below me and to my left ran the indigo river, striped with white where the water was ripped by rocks.

Once back down along the river, scuffing along the barren rock shelves, it was not hard to know when to turn inland to inspect one of the two campsites along this stretch. As soon as I saw the shiny spoor of the aluminum canoe ground into the granite along shore, I knew a camp was near. These camps were fairly clean and both were lovely, hunched beneath the jack pines and kissed by water.

The river turned sharply south and a little west even though it is generally heading east to the upper falls. After cleaning site #3, I stayed along the high banks in the forest, watching as the river gradually grew wider and flat. I glanced up and I caught something unusual through the trees: a horizontal line.

Horizontal lines are not common in the jackstraw architecture of nature. Except for the horizon of lakes or plains, little in the wild runs flat. I learned this many years ago when deer hunting the thick northern forest of Minnesota. "Look for horizontal lines," said an old-timer when asked how he spotted deer in heavy cover. "Nothin' natural in these woods is flat, ceptin' maybe a deer's back."

Well, nothing except a deer, or maybe a moose or bear. But I knew what he meant and remembered it. But what I saw was neither a deer, nor a moose. I was seeing a cable, a wrist-thick strand of twisted steel, and a small cable car, hanging on wheels. The cable spanned the entire river, dipping slightly over the middle.

It was then I remembered reading the stories of Bill Magie, a relatively recent explorer of the canoe country and a man I wish I had met. Magie died in 1982.

Magie was described by Bob Cary, editor of the Ely Echo newspaper, as "that irreverent, irascible leprechaun of the border lakes." He was that, and much more.

Magie was a wilderness guide of some fame and one of the major forces in the battle to set this area aside as a motorless wilderness. Though not as poetic or as well known as his contemporary, Sigurd Olson, Magie's love for this country was unmatched. From the time of his youth Magie found the lure of canoe country irresistible and spent much of his life exploring it. Though well educated and born of a wealthy family, Magie took every opportunity to live and work along the border. Over the years he did survey work, guided and cruised timber.

It was during his survey years that Magie built this very cable car over the Basswood River in 1928. Charged with monitoring water levels and current flow, Magie found the ice too dangerous in this area to be trusted in the winter, the time of normal measurements. Rather than drilling a hole in the ice to check flow, the alternate method of an aerial trolley was used, allowing the surveyor access to the main current safely from above.

And so it sits yet. Although the construction of such a system would be out of the question today, a ban on any type of permanent or mechanical artifice in place, I looked at the cable car as a link with someone I would have liked to have known. Here was a tie to a man who had known the canoe country the way I hoped I would, intimately and over long years. During Magie's early explorations they rarely saw tourists. Indeed, one was more likely to run into some of the few Indians that still made this area home. A more wild land then, with few maps and many unnamed places on those charts, it afforded an even darker, more mysterious sense of freedom than it does today. There is a quality about the unknown that brings excitement and adventure to the surface and though the canoe country is still wild, knowing that it is well mapped and that few places have gone unseen by the explorer's prying eyes tames it to a degree.

I felt other links to Magie. Due to his extended outings along the border, and the difficulty of providing food for his survey crews, Magie had obtained a permit from the Premier of Ontario to kill what meat (primarily moose) was necessary to feed his crews. Decked out with official seals and colors, Magie described that "It looked like a passport to heaven or somethin'!"

Magie kept that permit for many years and I could sense in his stories the pride he had in that piece of paper. To him it meant freedom, one less constriction forced upon those in the wilderness by governments. It meant they could live a bit closer to the land, use what was needed to survive. It was one less string attached, one more tentacle of civilization sheared away, for a man with the skill and the right to hunt in this country could stretch his trips out longer.

In my pocket I was carrying a piece of paper from the Canadian government as well. No, it was not a permit to shoot a moose or any other game, but it meant as much to me.

Stamped with the seal of Canadian Customs at Prairie Portage, it was an unusual seasonal, daily customs clearance that allowed Mary Jo and I to make short forays into Canada. Without this the rivers and bays along our territory, within sight and smell, would have been off limits, illegal to explore. Under "Highway Route" was written in "Crooked Lake" and our vehicle was listed as "1 Canoe, 2 people."

I felt about this as Magie must have felt about his permit. It represented freedom and a sense of belonging to this land. Like the Indians, voyageurs and men like Magie, we were not constrained overly by the imaginary line that separated the two halves of the canoe country.

I turned into the forest and decided to cut cross country to the portage. At first I could easily follow an old blazed trail through the woods but I soon became confused. The old marks hacked into the jack pines had faded to grey and were virtually indistinguishable from the bark of the trees. Some of the trees so marked had also blown over or had fallen with age, leaving gaps in the clues. Crossing large lichen carpeted granite openings, I was not sure at which end I would find another blaze, making the choices even more confusing.

It was at one such point I grew thoroughly disoriented. I knew that I could not truly get lost since the river flowed to the east and I only needed to make for it to regain my bearings. But I had been gone long now and was late for my rendevous with Mary Jo. Going back to the river would add to the delay.

If you have ever been turned around in country with which you are not familiar, you know the sudden tightness in your chest which wells up, the quick spasm of panic. Though I wasn't lost, I certainly didn't know exactly where I was either. It is a fine line.

I decided to sit down and have, in Magie fashion, a conference with myself.

Looking around at the lay of the land I searched for what would be a logical path. If this was Magie's trail, the one they had used to come back and periodically check the current flows, it would be one that afforded the easiest, if not the most direct, access. I guessed that even though I needed to head south and west to hit the portage, the hogback ridge of granite on which I sat in the sweltering sun, which ran southeast, would provide the easiest travel. I followed it.

Halfway down the ridge I came to a cairn, a small pile of rocks that marks trails where there are no trees to blaze. I knew then I was on the trail of Bill Magie and followed the ridge to the end, searching for the first blaze. I found it on a fallen pine. From then on, though I lost the trail momentarily once or twice, it was a short time and a direct line to the portage.

Gypsy told me Mary Jo had been up the portage, her tail wagging at her scent. I followed Gypsy to Mary Jo, who was looking for me after growing weary with my tardiness. The three of us walked to the upper falls to have lunch.

I told Mary Jo of my little adventure, of how I had found Magie's cable car and trail. She looked concerned that I had gotten turned around because, as she said "If you got lost who'd find you? After all, you *are* the ranger." It would have been embarrassing.

Still, I was excited that I had found what I did. You might think it a matter of less importance, but I enjoy trying to connect with those of the past whom I admire. I have more than once followed Sigurd Olson's path, planning obscure canoe routes from the very telltale clues he may have left in a story. There is some satisfaction in pitching your tent where he had.

And today I felt a link with someone else I admired. Though in fact we never met, today our paths had crossed. I had been on the trail of Bill Magie. I liked that.

Paddled to north end of Wednesday Bay to begin our eagle survey. Found and observed eagle nests 60E, 61E, 321E and 62E. Only 321E is occupied. Two adults spotted in or near 321E but no young observed. Thank goodness the biologist had marked the nest locations so clearly on our map or it may have been very difficult to spot them.

Thoroughly cleaned site #26, Wednesday Bay. "Dan'l Boone" types had camped here. We found bough beds, trenching around tent sites and hot coals in firegrate.

The sky had the look of rain most of the day but we were fortunate it didn't deliver.

◆ OF EAGLES AND MOOSE ◆

It wasn't until I had drunk deeply of the water just offshore of the eagle nest that I spotted it. Pink and round, it lay in two feet of water, almost immediately beneath the pine that harbored the empty nest. A very dead, very bloated, moose.

We approached it cautiously, not because there is much to fear from a dead moose but because such scenes can be very ugly. When we were ten feet away we decided we were near enough and caught the odor to prove it. But we hadn't been the first to find this moose.

Obviously there had been many animals and birds making use of this carcass since it had washed ashore. There are many turkey vultures and ravens in the area and we could see sign of their feeding on the rotting flesh. Most likely the very eagles we sought on this survey had also found this carcass to be of use. Maybe this moose, so near to the nest, was one reason they had decided not to occupy it this year. While a handy supply of food just downstairs might be considered a blessing to some, the other predatory and scavenger birds attracted by it might make egg laying and chick rearing in this locale an iffy thing at best.

What had happened to this moose? The only predators they need worry about are wolves and if the wolves had been responsible for this kill, there would be no carcass left to float and bloat. At this time of the year moose find life pretty easy and there likely was no reason for one to die. Wolves are primarily a threat in the winter when the deep snows aid them in catching and successfully bringing down a moose. There is little chance of a moose drowning either since the hair of their coat is hollow. Moose float like a cork.

No, this moose had probably been a victim of treacherous ice conditions last winter, dangerous ice for which Crooked Lake is known.

Old timers always stayed clear of Crooked Lake during the winter, even throughout the coldest spells. I have heard that there was a winter trail through the forest to the south of the lake, skirting most of its length so that a man on snowshoe or by dog team would not have to risk death on thin ice. Crooked is more like a giant river than a lake, especially in narrow areas, with many currents snaking through its length. There are spots on this lake that actually have currents so strong they approach rapids. If you ever get lost on Crooked, look for a narrows between islands. The water plants flow there with the current and they always dip their heads to the west.

Because of these currents the ice is dangerously thin in spots, even at forty below zero. Had this moose wandered out onto such thin ice? At near a thousand pounds live weight, it takes a lot of ice to hold a full grown moose.

It is easy to let your mind wander to that day, the moose moving across the brilliant white of the lake from the dark spruce shore. Perhaps there was some choice browse across the lake that held its interest. Maybe wolves were involved, flushing the giant deer from the forest in a frantic effort to escape. Whatever the reason for its last journey, at some point the ice gave way, plunging the moose into the frigid waters.

If it was lucky the moose might have come up under solid ice after breaking through, making the end relatively quick. A short struggle, a gasp for breath and then the water rushing into its lungs. Death.

If the moose was unlucky it broke through and remained floating in its own hole, unable to crawl back out or break ice to shore. Ice that may not hold your weight from above is many times harder to break on edge. And sharp.

How long did this moose struggle to stay afloat? Did it cut itself on the jagged ice trying to push its way through? Obviously the water was over its head or it could have used the purchase of good footing to bulk its way through the ice to the safety of land. Even a powerful moose would have trouble with breaking ice while swimming. Death in this case would be slow and miserable.

It is also easy to imagine yourself in the same scenario, the terror you would feel, the hopelessness. Do moose feel? I wonder. They must at least feel the fear, if not the despair. Nature, they say, is cruel.

When the ice melted, this moose, now long dead, began a new role. The eagles and vultures, returning after the long winter, must have found the moose quickly once it washed to shore. Though the death of this moose might have been meaningless, it was not without consequence. Now it provided a needed supply of food for these birds at a time when they were tired from migrating, at a time when they were stressed from nesting.

One moose, more or less, would not harm the moose population around Crooked Lake. One moose, more or less, would not assure or ruin the chances of survival for nesting eagles. But no moose might. With no moose (or deer, or caribou) the other creatures that call this place home could be seriously affected. We know moose are critical to the survival of the wolves. But what about the other creatures?

When you look at the death of this moose on the small scale it seems cruel and unimportant. But when you look at it on the large scale, its death was necessary. No creature, not even man, exists in a vacuum. The eagles we cherish don't just exist. They don't eat worms. They eat flesh and sometimes it may be the flesh of moose. Whether moose meat is an important item in its diet, I'm not sure. I doubt it. But a meal of moose, at just the right time, after the long migration or while trying to incubate eggs, just might be critical to an individual eagle.

If you look at the eagle nests in this area you may begin wondering if moose meat, or other winter kills that wash up, might have been a factor in their location. In Wednesday Bay alone there are four eagle nests, all on the Canadian shore. Both entering and leaving Wednesday Bay are spots where the lake narrows to just a few yards, and through which pulse powerful currents. If your diet depended partially upon such winter kills, Wednesday Bay would be a good spot to set up house.

More than falling into a lake or river, this moose fell into the biotic stream. Ugly as it was lying there bloated, it has given life and strength to many other creatures.

I only wish I hadn't taken a drink just downstream of it.

The eagle nest just above the moose carcass was unoccupied. It also looked to be in disrepair. While we have seen the eagles that frequent Lower Basswood Falls, we were disappointed not to find these birds at home. Eagles often have more than one nest and may spend alternate years in each so we still hoped to find them in one of the others.

But it was time for lunch. The campsite just across from this nest looked equally empty and since we had not had a chance to check on it yet, we decided to do so.

This site is well hidden behind a big mound of precambrian rock. Because of this rock, the usually visible signs of a landing are masked. But it is a campsite nonetheless and we probably would have guessed so even without a red dot marking its location on our map. After you spend enough time in the canoe country you can pick a likely camp spot for some distance. Any areas of rock are always worth investigating.

When we pulled up beneath the rock I instantly smelled woodsmoke. Maybe I had been wrong. Perhaps someone was camped here. I gave a friendly "hulloo".

The rock mound shielded our view of the interior of the camp but as we received no reply, we beached the canoe and scrambled up the rock face. It felt good to stretch.

A campfire was burning in the deserted camp. On the tent site was a mound of balsam boughs and behind it we found the naked stump of the tree from which they were cut. The trunk of the tree had been pitched back into the bushes.

A deep trench had been cut into the soil around where their tent had been.

I shook my head. No matter how many times we see it, Mary Jo and I have a hard time believing in just what condition people will leave a campsite.

Before lunch Mary Jo and I repaired what we could and cleaned up the rest.

Lunches for us are simple. We had yet to run out of fresh bread and when we would, we planned to bake. Usually though we rely on hard crackers on canoe trips, planning the same for this adventure, and with it goes cheese and salami, as well as a water bottle of fruit drink mixed from powdered concentrate. Good cheese is not hard to find these days but we have found that real hard salami, the kind that is smoked thoroughly to avoid spoiling, is more difficult to locate. The supermarket types in their bright shrink wrapped packages usually have too high a fat content and rarely keep well without refrigeration. We have found, however, a real old fashioned butcher shop that still smokes their own and also carries imported meats cured the old country way. These sausages will keep up to ten days with no chilling making a delicious and easy lunch on the trail.

A handful of gorp or a few caramels and a couple of minutes of inspecting the inside of our eyelids ends our noon-time ritual on the trail.

When we left the site it was clean and ready for the next campers. Maid service, Mary Jo reiterated.

The day was cool, perhaps because there was a good breeze from the northwest and a lightly overcast sky. On this section of Crooked Lake it is not difficult to stay out of the wind because the lake is so sinuous. There is always a lee shore and the crossings where you might be caught by the wind are short. Wednesday Bay is shallow though in its center and when the wind does blow, it can quickly build a good sea.

Today we were fortunate to have the wind at our back. Though we have been out here a short time, we are already building strong paddling muscles as well as rounding off the rough spots in our technique. We find that twenty short, rapid strokes to a side, then a quick switch at the call of Hut!, is a pace we can keep up for hours and miles. We travel at a fast pace (for canoeists, that is), but most of life these past days has never exceeded five miles an hour. It is a pace that I find to my liking.

Heading south from this site, and the bloated moose, there is a long rock promontory punching into the bay. I have learned from reading the tales of Bill Magie that this spot is known as Pancake Point. According to Magie, the Candadian Rangers used to meet here to conduct business and socialize. They also held a pancake eating contest. I would have liked to have seen that.

The next eagle nest south is on a point just opposite Table Rock. It too was empty. However, the camp at Table Rock was not and we waved at the party as we passed by.

Table Rock was also an important meeting place, but not for rangers. No, long before this area was divided up into countries and managed by governments, Table Rock saw sometimes large gatherings. It was a meeting place for the Ojibway and Sioux. The Voyageurs often camped here after making the treacherous journey down the Basswood River. It was a logical spot to pick up an Indian guide if the party was not familiar with the wanderings of Crooked Lake. But it served a more important purpose.

Table Rock is named for a large slab of stone that sits near the water's edge. Dropped by a receding glacier, this flat slab was just the right size and height for use by the Voyageurs in repairing any damage done to their birch bark canoes during the descent down the river. On this rock they rolled the canoes over and while dinner was being prepared, they could heat some pitch and seal any leaks. This was a frequent ritual for these travelers and a critical step in keeping both trade goods and lives safe.

The rock now is broken, cracked down its width. According to Bill Magie it was broken in an attempt to move it to a museum during the logging era. What a ridiculous thing to do.

If you were to paddle east-northeast from the tip of Table Rock you would come to a sand beach along the Canadian shore. It is above this beach that a most impressive eagle nest sits, well back on the hillside, in a large white pine. Locating this nest was easy because of the bright white head of the eagle that sat on its edge. Mary Jo and I took turns sharing the binoculars, watching this handsome bird. Even with the binoculars we could not tell if there were young ones in the nest or whether the eagle was actually sitting on eggs. The nest was so big, and deep, that I had the feeling that anything down in its hollow center would have to be very large before it could peek over the top.

The eagle watched us unconcernedly, gazing first left then right. At one point it moved as if to change positions and flapped its wings to maintain balance. Thinking we might be beginning to disturb it, and not wanting to cause it to leave its eggs or young unattended, we paddled down the shore to the last eagle nest in Wednesday Bay.

Having found the eagle in the nest we had just left, we had no doubt that the last one would be empty. We did see midway between the two nests, sitting in a lightning shattered white pine, another eagle. Perhaps the mate of the first, it was only a few hundred yards to the south. The last nest was indeed empty, as we had expected.

Eagles lend a majesty to any landscape. Though the day was grey and overcast, their white heads and tails seemed lit from within. It is hard to put a value on the sighting of an eagle but there is little doubt that the canoe country would seem a poorer place without their presence. The eagles are making a comeback now after becoming dangerously rare during the '60's and '70's. Once the pesticide DDT was banned the eagles began to recover and now each year their numbers grow and their range expands.

Here, where such dangerous chemicals were never used, it is hard to imagine the creatures that make it home could have been endangered. But make no mistake about it, whatever happens in the world outside this sanctuary of the past has a direct bearing. Though there is a boundary drawn about the canoe country, it is only on paper. It is permeable. Mosquito control in the suburbs of America can come to roost here. And it will, when birds no longer do.

The least ripple in the center of a pond eventually reaches the furthest shore.

As we watched, the eagle in the pine swooped from its roost and glided out over the bay. When it would turn to one side or the other the white of its head and tail flashed white, even in the poor light of this cloudy day. We followed it with our eyes until it circled back toward the hillside of its roost, climbing and then eventually disappearing behind the hill. Already he was over Robinson Lake, could see the seldom visited Round and Lost Lakes. I envied him his ease and wondered what it would be like to feel the lift of wind under your wings, the thrill and power of a full dive.

An interesting encounter occurred as we headed back to the cabin. Just south of the narrow entrance to Wednesday Bay we talked to a group of six men who had paused to fish. They reported to us that when they had stopped at an island campsite in Friday Bay they found it littered with nearly one hundred dead fish on shore and more in the water. I questioned them as to whether the fish had been whole, or cleaned, knowing this would be the first step in determining whether the fish kill had a natural cause or not. None of them recalled taking notice.

We thanked them for the information and rode the tail wind back to the falls. As we paddled I wondered what had happened at the campsite. Since we were scheduled to make a trip there in just a few days, I let it ride. The fish were dead and the camp deserted. There would be little we could do.

We had found the eagles of Wednesday Bay today and a very dead moose. What, I wondered, would we find in Friday Bay? I feared I could already guess. We paddled silently back to the cabin, the only words exchanged were the Huts! punctuating silent counts of twenties.

Thunderstorms kept us off the lake most of the day. Cleaned and repaired cabin.

When the weather finally broke we thoroughly cleaned the two campsites near the cabin.

Later, as Gypsy and I walked along the river, I was startled to see a great blue heron standing many yards back from shore in dense forest. I had never heard of herons doing such a thing. When he spotted us he did his best imitation of a popple sapling.

◆ THE CABIN ◆

Sixty-four, sixty-five, sixty-six. I sat crouched beneath the north window of the kitchen, counting the rings in the exposed end of a pine log that formed our walls. This log of our new home was sixty-six years old when felled. Others ranged from fifty to seventy years of age when they were transformed from a wall of dark timber to a wall of a cabin.

If this cabin was built in the 1930's, as we had been told, then the trees that form it were seedlings during the 1860's and '70's. Dead though they were, we were surrounded by trees of over one hundred years in age.

When those trees were growing this place would have been somewhat different. The caribou, the indigenous deer of this region, would still have been here, perhaps in great numbers since the logging that changed their habitat had not yet taken place. Stands of mature white and Norway pines would have been plentiful and while the canoe country is still very beautiful in its second growth of birch, poplar and fir, it must have been enchanting in those dark climax pine forests. The moccasin prints of the Ojibway would still be visible on the portage trails and those people, had you the opportunity to sit and

talk with them, could have told you first hand about the passing of the Voyageurs, for the last brigades passed this way not too long before the mid-point of that century. The American Fur Company operated in this region until 1842 when the depression of 1837 and the change in the fashion of men's hats, which no longer required beaver pelts, caused their empire to collapse. No doubt a few hearty traders plied these waterways for some time to come. The last fur trade post of the Lake Superior region, the Hudson Bay Company's Michipicoten House, closed its doors in 1904.

If you had been here then you might have sat on the rock point on the American side of the falls and watched the expanse toward Crooked Lake in hopes of spotting the fiesty Voyageurs. What would you give to have spotted those flashing paddles, red bowed canoes and gayly colored sashes as they first appeared to your sight near the pictured rocks? Had the wind been right you might have even heard them first as their deep male voices kept rhythm with the swinging paddles, singing the happy chansons.

I got to know our cabin well this day. Part of our job, we had been told, was to try to undo some of the neglect it had seen. Though it had been built square and strong some fifty years ago, time has taken its toll. Its maintenance has been lacking as the Forest Service decides the cabin's fate. In general, the Forest Service frowns on permanent structures in a wilderness area, even their own, and because of that indecision the old cabin, built long before the canoe country's designation as an official wilderness and the coming of rules governing the use of such structures, sits often unused and ill-cared for.

Sagging has left a gap along the joint where the hardwood floors join the log walls. Mary Jo handed down to me strips of the sticky, smelly oakum, a "rope" of sorts impregnated with a tar-like substance, as I crawled along wedging it into the cracks with a whittled down piece of wood. When the floor joints were sealed against drafts and mosquitoes, we did the same to the cracks around doors and windows, finishing up by plugging those openings that have appeared near the eaves.

Our little home is quite compact. The cabin is twenty-eight feet long by eighteen feet wide and has two entrances, one each to the north and south. The south entrance opens into the kitchen. As you step inside there is a wood fired cookstove to your right, which, because it lacks a stovepipe, is unusable. To the left of the door is a sink. It is an unusual sink in that it drains onto the floor, where we placed a bucket beneath the lonely drain pipe. A small table, two chairs, a bench and a hutch complete the furnishings.

The bedroom, entered by a door from the kitchen on the north end, is the bigger of the two rooms at fifteen feet wide. It contains two bunk beds and each of the four bunks comes complete with mattresses that show that the mice have discovered that foam also makes good insulation for their nests. They have carted off parts of each mattress.

There is also a small table, desk-like, that separates the bunks as well as a metal closet, which is mouse-proof. Completing the opulent decor is a rusty wood stove used for heat and a wooden box (the final resting place of one smelly little mouse) for firewood.

Another door exits the cabin north from the bedroom and onto a little covered porch. The porch is on a separate foundation which has sagged away from the cabin, leaving the roof at crazy angles. Most of the windows in the building are no longer rectangular but are parallelograms, meaning they will not yield to our attempts to open them. We did find, however, enough windows that still work, mostly on the east and west walls, to provide ventilation and I transferred the better window screens to them.

All in all, we like this place. Despite it being rustic and lacking maintenance, it is still snug and comfortable. A bed, of any kind, is luxurious in this country and being able to cook and eat indoors seems almost decadent. We do all of our cooking on a two burner Coleman stove, bake in a folding Coleman oven atop the stove and use gas lanterns for light. Our water comes from the river, just thirty steps from the north door and we even have our own box latrine back in the bushes.

While I tightened up cracks and fixed windows and doors, Mary Jo began to make things feel like home. She scrubbed and cleaned, hung maps and a calendar on the walls and located pegs in dark corners to hang clothing. A good sweeping and clean windows made the place feel friendlier. Arranged on the table in the bedroom were our numerous books, both of us being voracious readers. Hats were hung on pegs, coffee cups placed on the shelves and our moccasins tucked under the bed. By the time we were done, we felt very much at home.

We decided, though, not to use the cabinets to store our precious supply of food. The wooden hutch showed much sign of visitations by mice and nearly every door on it had evidence of their toothy determination. We left our food in the unique fiberglas food packs, "wanigans" as they are called, supplied to us by the Forest Service. Gypsy had already found out that if she left any of her dog food in her dish, it would not take long for it to disappear. She spends much time staring at a mouse hole by the kitchen door, cat-like, and I'm sure she'll catch one of the little thieves before we leave.

Just what does one need to be comfortable? A warm bed, a place to keep dry, food and clothing seem enough to meet our needs. Our books are our only luxury, except for the artificial light by which we read and write. Our water is pure and is brought daily past our door, ever fresh and plentiful. Chickadees, loons and owls provide our music, except for our own humming and whistling which we find ourselves unconsciously doing. We have been satisfied with less on many a canoe trip but we also realize that the nearly three months out here will be made easier by the comfort of this little cabin.

I have found that on canoe trips the bonds to civilization take at least a week to stretch and snap. Until that time has passed, one finds himself longing, perhaps subconsciously, for the comforts of home; a shower, a soft bed, and for those of us with bad backs, an honest to goodness chair. When the limits of our softness are finally severed, we settle down into a life that finds its needs in the precious surroundings about us. The shower becomes less important, although keeping reasonably clean does not. The sleeping bag in the tent calls as invitingly as has any bed. Simple food and clear water meet our needs and strengthen our bodies. When this transition has taken place, and only then, one can finally begin to appreciate wild places on a meaningful level.

I'm looking forward to that final transition now. The worries of closing up our home, making arrangements for my business and tying up the hundreds of loose ends I encountered as I prepared for this trip still sit near the front of my mind. There are worries too about our new job. We do want to do it right. Although we are volunteers, we are taking this position as seriously as any job we have ever held.

Until that time comes when the Crooked Lake cabin becomes home, until we think of getting up and going to work as slipping into our canoe and paddling down the lake, I will be a bit uneasy. But from long experience in the canoe country I know that the shift will come soon, for the more often one experiences it, the quicker it comes back. And I will not be aware of my settling down, but will one day just have it dawn upon me that for a long time I have not thought of showers, pizza, and traffic.

When that time comes I will be a happy man.

Thunderstorms on and off all day forcing us to stay off the water.

Made contact with the group in site below cabin that arrived late last night. They were all young adults from Chicago. Arrived to much yelling and screaming which was repeated this morning. Had cut live cedars for firewood and had banned cans in possession.

Just before dinner the weather finally cleared and feeling the need, we went for a swim. Lordy, but that water is cold!

◆ GREEN WOOD DOESN'T BURN ◆

Morning came as the night had fallen, noisily. We awoke to the same raucous screaming that we had heard about bed time and which I had been too tired to check out. Because of the nasty weather today, black thunderheads moving in rapidly from the west, we delayed any plans for water travel and instead I took a walk with Gypsy to the campsite below the cabin, from which the noise had emanated.

I don't know for how many hundreds of years this site has been a favorite camping spot and its popularity certainly hasn't waned. It is has been occupied every night since we arrived and for good reason. Its proximity to the cascades and the canopy of huge pines makes it a particularly beautiful spot.

Today there was a group of young adults camped here, three men and three women. They were a happy, albeit noisy party and when I appeared in their camp they were friendly and anxious to ask questions. Gypsy found the dog lover in the party, of which there is at least always one, and settled down to have her ears scratched.

Breakfast was cooking and the coffee was on as we made our introductions. I found out they were from Chicago and only one of them had ever been on a canoe trip before. The group was organized after someone had picked up a brochure from an Ely outfitter at a sport show in the Chicago area.

I scanned the campsite, as I had begun to do out of habit, to look for anything amiss. I did not have to look long. A can of shortening sat on a rock next to the firegrate and limbs from a cedar tree, still bearing green foliage, lay in a pile next it. The fire was sputtering weakly.

"Green wood doesn't burn so well, does it?" I posed in a round about way to approach the situation.

"Thought it was dead," said the man with the axe.

I looked around and spotted just twenty feet distant the raw wounds on an otherwise healthy cedar where the branches had been hacked away. What could I say?

I explained to them that it was illegal to cut live trees and that cans were not allowed. They look stunned and remorseful and went on to say that it was dark when they had arrived and they had wanted to cook something to eat, hence the hurried hunt in the dark for wood to burn. How they came to have a can in possession I do not know for the area outfitters are good about adhering to this rule.

"Don't you have a camp stove?" I queried.

The axe man hustled to a pack and withdrew a compact campstove and trotted back, proud of his possession. He quickly gave me the run-down on the stove, how he had purchased it just for this trip. He had, he explained, researched all the stoves on the market and had decided this was by far the best. He quoted boiling times, BTU's and fuel capacity.

I grinned and said it was a nice stove, the same one that we use on the trail. I also spent some time explaining the reasons they should have used it last night, why cutting down live trees is wrong and how they could go about finding dead wood when they needed it. And I suggested that they no longer bring cans into the wilderness area.

I wanted to say more, but couldn't. I wanted to do more, but was unable. As volunteer wilderness rangers we had absolutely no power to enforce the laws.

What I wanted to say was that I wished this man, who so gleefully researched the stoves and had ignorantly scarred a tree had spent an equal amount of time reading the regulations on the back of his permit. That he should try spending a like effort on reading about wilderness ethics as he does being another consumer. If each one of us spent a few hours less time scrambling to earn more money to buy more things and used that scavenged time to learn just the tiniest bit about the natural world we are each a part of, both the world, and ourselves would be much the better.

Instead, we took a walk down the shore past the boathouse. I helped him gather some dead wood, the abundant "squaw" wood that requires neither axe nor saw, and upon returning to the camp, demonstrated how these thumb to wrist size pieces can be used for cooking, the size helping to regulate the fire's temperature.

I left them as the thunderstorm broke, huddled under their tarp, eating breakfast. Hopefully the time spent with them had not been wasted and that they would treat the canoe country more kindly from now on.

Mary Jo had a hot pot of coffee waiting in the snug cabin. Gypsy and I had delayed our return just long enough to be caught by the driving rain. We were fairly soaked after we had scurried up the trail. I poured a cup of coffee and put on a dry shirt. The rain pelted the windows and the spruce trees to the west shook with the storm's fury. Out on the bay I could see the little wind devils, miniature twisters, whipping down the bay in battalions, assaulting the granite shore. This storm was no major battle destined to erode the granite knob. Water has time. Though the rains would dash themselves on the rocks of the canoe country with no apparent effect, with eons they would change the face of the land.

Paddling would be out of the question until this weather broke. I looked around the cabin for projects that could be done indoors and could see many. It was going to be a lazy day indoors at Lower Basswood Falls.

Mary Jo and I left the cabin at 8:40 a.m. and reached campsite #2 in Sunday Bay about 3:30 p.m. Since that site was occupied and the seas were running two to three feet in Sunday Bay we turned and rode waves to a site north of Saturday Bay, arriving about 4:30.

We were quite surprised to see three deer today, all feeding in shallow water along the shores of Wednesday Bay. Their summer coats are such a beautiful shade of red. Two of the deer were bucks with antlers thick in velvet.

Along the way we stopped and cleaned site #19 near Big Current and observed an osprey nest nearby. There was one adult in the nest but no offspring were visible, which is not surprising since the nest appeared to be five feet deep. We watched as another adult osprey delivered a northern pike nearly four pounds in size to the nest.

Wind strong all day. Thunderstorms drove us to shore in Friday Bay where we ate lunch while hiding beneath a hastily spread tarp.

We are both quite weary this evening.

◆ WILD RIDE ◆

Slate grey curtains slanted down all around us as we turned north into Sunday Bay and as they rippled in the wind they revealed fleeting blue patches of sky. We had been fortunate so far this day to escape most of the thunderstorms passing through but were forced to sit patiently beneath a tarp on Friday Bay as one particularly vicious storm rattled by. It looked as though our luck might hold out a bit longer and allow us to cross Sunday Bay to the island campsite we hoped to use.

I quickly adjusted our load, especially the awkward bundle of tools, to ride as low as possible in the canoe. Whitecaps were rolling down the length of the bay and I knew once we were into the full force of the wind there would be no margin for error.

Although the day had been windy, WNW winds of twenty miles per hour or more, we had been able to hug the shore of twisting Crooked Lake or, at least, dart from island to island. Paddling into the wind as we had for the last five hours had drained us but with the island campsite in view just a half mile away, we paddled out into the gale with renewed vigor.

"Get Gypsy to lie down, Mary Jo. This is going to be a wild ride. Don't switch sides until I say so, we may not be able to switch on twenty strokes."

"I don't like this, Michael."

"It'll be OK, Hon. We've paddled in worse. Remember Sturgeon Lake?"

I'm quite sure she did. The year before we had disappeared for a month to explore the Quetico and two of those twenty-nine days were spent battling big seas on huge Sturgeon Lake. Windbound on the north shore the second day, we were frustrated by the knowledge that the southerly side, the lee shore, would make for easy traveling on this windy but otherwise beautiful day. Spurning breakfast for an early start when we saw the whitecaps building at dawn, we broke camp quickly and headed south. Halfway across we were forced down to our knees to lower our center of gravity and we paddled mightily for an hour, finally reaching a calm bay.

It really is quite difficult to paddle when you're holding your breath in spasms of fright.

It had been, though, a very good experience for each time we test ourselves in the waves we learn more about just what we, and our canoe, can handle. With each experience we have become less afraid to challenge rough water, within reason, and I have found myself enjoying the wind and the spray.

The problem today was this: the island was due west and the waves were running north and south. Paddling in the troughs would be foolhardy so I turned the bow into the wind as we rounded the last bend on the northerly, Canadian shore. If we were lucky we could paddle north and ferry west at the same time.

It is a difficult moment when you realize that you may have bitten off more than you can chew, especially when that bite involves not only you but someone you love very much. We fought our way into the open channel, the bow of the canoe rising on each wave and slapping water upon falling as the crest slid beneath the mid-point of the canoe. We were a very dangerous teeter-totter. The island loomed as an oasis of safety to our left and the Canadian shore, pounded with surf, roared in white spray to the right. Halfway to the island, there was no way we could turn back. A canoe would broach in seconds if caught by the wind. I could feel my strength waning and knew Mary Jo was in trouble.

"Switch!" she cried. "I have to switch sides!"

"On Hut! then," I hollered into the wind. "One, two, three, Hut!"

Quickly we swapped paddling sides. It was only a few strokes before I realized that I could gather no momentum paddling on this side, every stroke either a J or a draw to keep the bow from turning downwind. We would have to switch back to the other side and stay there, with only short breaks such as this. I called the Hut.

Slowly we were crawling north and west, minute by tiring minute, although we were not moving laterally as much as I would have liked. If we went too far north we would miss the island and be forced to turn in the roughest of water or continue on to the far end of Sunday Bay, neither being a particularly palatable prospect.

Our Stewart River canoe was built for just such conditions, having the round bottom, high freeboard and sweeping bows of the famous Chestnut Cruiser from which it was designed. Harkening back to the days when canoe travelers did not sit out any but the worst weather and carried heavy loads deep into the bush, this canoe would handle waves that would turn many modern straight, shallow and low bowed canoes into submarines. Nonetheless, spray washed occasionally over the bow and while we were in no danger of swamping yet, we all began to get damp. Gypsy lay stoically in the bow, just her nose pointing skyward on the deck. She didn't move and she knew she had better not for she also knew the thwack of a canoe paddle for dogs that move in a canoe. My arms ached with the exertion, especially because we could not switch sides every twenty strokes as we were used to doing, and I admired Mary Jo for her persistence. One could simply not quit in this situation, and she knew it. There was no question I could count on her to give it her all. No greater comfort is there than this type of unquestioned faith in your partner.

The target campsite is on the south end of the island and we were well north of it now, approaching the northern tip. Waves beat furiously on the island and boiled over rocks and reefs offshore. We slowed our paddling as I tried to scull the canoe sideways toward the island, just enough forward momentum maintained to keep the bow into the wind. At last we were nearer the island than the mainland. We would still have to turn the canoe downwind, but at least we might be able to do it in the somewhat calmer waters offshore the island.

"When I call Hut, switch fast, draw hard and then paddle like hell," I bellowed. "Ready? Hut!"

Digging in furiously we swung the canoe on the top of a wave I had been watching. As the wave passed beneath us the perfectly rockered canoe pivoted effortlessly and with a gasp from both of us we were quartering downwind, heading for the campsite.

We shot into the gap between this island and the one to its south, riding the surf. White combers hissed down the length of the canoe and I watched as they inched upward toward the gunwales amidship. We had a good two inches to spare. In the calm behind the island we breathed deeply and looked around. Much to our dismay a group was occupying the campsite. We chatted briefly with them as we munched granola bars to stave our hunger. I debated with myself what we would do next as we floated in the calm of the island's lee, our map across my knees. Heading north was impossible and the waves were even bigger to the south and west of the island. The campsite at the bottom of Sunday Bay would be hard to reach and if it too was occupied we would have no choice but to paddle north into the worst of the waves. It seemed risky.

Instead we headed south and east, darting from island to island toward Saturday Bay. With three campsites to choose from there, I felt optimistic one would be available.

Finally, at 4:30, we rounded the tip of a large island and spotted an open campsite. The whole area was lit as if by a spotlight, the clouds torn just enough to allow the sun through the rent. It was a relief to just set foot on shore again. Mary Jo was tired and shaken and we broke out the food pack before starting to set up camp. We've learned from long experience that everything looks brighter when your blood-sugar isn't low. We felt much better for the snack.

While Mary Jo rested I walked around the camp to stretch my canoe-cramped legs. In a short time I had a mound of garbage piled off to one side, left for us by some thoughtless campers. It included a minnow bucket (broken, of course), one 4'x4'x8' chicken wire fish box (for keeping fish alive), numerous film boxes and canisters (from the film used to capture the beauty of the area), miscellaneous litter and a picnic table made from pines hacked down.

It is a strange dichotomy. Today we witnessed the flawless grace of an osprey as it delivered, air-express, a four pound northern pike to its mate waiting in their nest. Though the weather was far from perfect, even sitting out the thunderstorm in Friday Bay under a tarp, eating our lunch, was enjoyable and each glimpse of blue through the soiled clouds was a cause to rejoice. The wind was strong and fresh and it both reddened our cheeks and tested our mettle as we struggled against it for seventeen or so miles.

All of this had been, in a sense, perfect, for even the adversity of wind is part of the fabric of a canoe trip.

And then you come across this. The mess and destruction we found within this perfect wilderness is left by only one species: homo sapien sloboni. The only scar upon the land is left by those who came here precisely because it is supposed to be pristine.

Mary Jo and I hauled the canoe up into the campsite and turned it over to use as a table. The weather was clearing now and while sunset was still hours away, our camp on the east end of the island behind the crest of a hill was growing dark beneath the pines. There was a chill to the air, born on northwest winds and magnified by our spray and sweat dampened clothing. A fire would feel good this evening.

While Mary Jo began dinner over the few scraps of firewood left us by the previous occupants I set up the tent and put our gear inside, returning to dismantle the ridiculous camp furniture. Some of it would make good firewood anyway.

In the pure darkness of a canoe country night, we sat around the fire, listening to the burning pine wood snap. Dinner was done, the dishes washed, the food pack hung safely high in the pines. I looked down at my hands. They were rough, red, chapped. When I flexed them they felt stiff and the notch between thumb and forefinger on my left hand was very tender to the touch, abused from repeated pressure from the canoe paddle. An amazing invention, the human hand. I don't often stop to consider them at home.

Gypsy snored softly behind the log I was leaning against. I watched as Mary Jo's head sunk once, twice, three times to her chest, only to snap back up in an attempt to stay awake.

"You tired, Mary Jo?"

"Mmmph?"

"Are you ready for bed, Hon?" I asked.

"If I can get up. Give me a hand."

I helped Mary Jo to her feet and while she and Gypsy crawled into the tent I walked around the camp, checking on things one last time before bed. Everything was snug, kindling was under the canoe and nothing that might be harmed by water should it rain during the night seemed to be left outside. I poured a bucket of water on the campfire, stirred the ashes and wetted it down again. The embers sputtered and hissed, steam rising to my face. The night grew blacker yet without the fire.

I straightened up and stretched my back muscles. If they were this stiff now, what would they be like in the morning?

It had been a wild ride in Sunday Bay.

We received no morning radio call due to poor reception. Tried to reach both Kawishiwi and the Lac La Croix cabin but could not make contact.

Continued working on the site we are in as well as sites #'s 3, 5 and 6. All required some work but none were in bad condition. Someone had trenched around the tent pad at #6, causing much erosion. We filled in trenching and tried to restore the area as much as possible.

Continued eagle survey in Saturday Bay. The nest there is apparently not being used this year.

The weather was warm and humid and the flies are absolutely atrocious. Found some good walleye fishing and kept a fine one for dinner.

◆ PAYMENT ◆

Gypsy looked relieved. We floated a hundred yards offshore our camp in the gathering darkness, she cool from a dip in the lake just before we departed. Laying across the centerline of the canoe, head resting on the gunwale, her eyes fought the urge to close. Finally gravity and slumber won and her head slid down the side of the canoe and came to rest on her paw. She was asleep.

The poor dog had reason to feel relieved. I have never seen the flies as bad as they were today, not in twenty-five years of summers in the canoe country. Droves of them followed us everywhere, even out onto the water, and when the wind would blow and we would hope for some relief, they would hide in the bowels of the boat, only to come back out when the wind lapsed. Small and dirty grey, they looked much like a common house fly. You could have no doubts when they bit for they did not sneak in and make off with a meal like a mosquito or black fly. Instead they bored through your skin with what felt like a red-hot poker. Gypsy took the brunt of their abuse for Mary Jo and I were protected somewhat by our clothing. Lying in the bottom of the canoe, and unable to move, she was a particularly tortured target. When we returned to camp after our day's work she trotted immediately to the tent and there was little question what she wanted. I unzipped the door and let her in. She curled up in a tight ball with a large sigh, glad to be away from the bugs. I had never seen her do that before.

This evening both she and I were enjoying the relative absence of insects and a cool, northwest breeze. All day the weather had been muggy and hot but with the dropping of the sun and the stirring of the slight breeze the air seemed to be relieved of the burden of moisture that had draped itself over our flesh all day. Mary Jo sat on a point on the island, reading a book and relaxing in the orange glow of sunset. It was a nearly perfect evening.

It would be a perfect evening, I thought, if I could just get the fish to bite. This island formed the southern shore of a channel, bounded on the north by an archipelago of smaller bits of land, all across from the international border. To my right lay Canada, to my left, the U.S.A.

This channel has been a good spot to fish for us in the past. A few years back I landed a northern pike here that I estimated was twenty-five pounds, hooking it on a small plug as we trolled for walleyes. Because Crooked Lake has a current moving from east to west and is relatively shallow, it is an incredibly fertile body of water for this country. Smallmouth bass, walleye and northern pike abound and it is not a difficult feat to catch fish here. Crooked is one lake that finds me always trailing a lure behind my canoe when we have the time to travel at a leisurely pace. You may not believe this but there have been times I've been forced to reel in that trailing lure because hooking so many fish slowed our progress.

Today we easily caught walleyes as we surveyed the eagle nest in Saturday Bay. Although we saw no sign of eagles at that spot, we hooked a number of walleyes while touring the area. Much of Saturday Bay is very shallow but where depth allowed, the walleyes congregated.

We finally kept one walleye of about four pounds and extended an invitation for him to join us for dinner. He was delicious.

A rock reef extended from the west end of a small island, a ridge of humped rocks just breaking the water. While it was a bit late in the year for good surface fishing for smallmouth bass, I tossed a floating plug near the rocks with hopeful anticipation, betting I might still be able to raise a fish from the depths. I did not have to wait long for as the little plug whirred along the surface (a streamlined lure with, believe it or not, a small propeller at the back that rotates on retrieve) a fish shattered the calm surface and attacked the plug. Incredibly, it missed the lure. A nice sized northern of five or six pounds, it arched its way above and across the plug. Back lit by the setting sun, the pike was a silhouette against the orange reflecting waters. Even as it flopped back into the lake I instinctively tried to set the hook, obviously to no avail. The plug flew through the air and landed with a splash near the canoe. Gypsy cracked open her eyes and gave me a "Hey! Keep it down. I'm trying to sleep" look.

With great leisure I paddled the canoe west into the light breeze, following the contours of the islands, drawn by the setting sun. A few small bass struck the lure and all were released unharmed. I could smell the fish scent on my hands. It smelled right; the clean, pleasant odor of fish from cool waters. I was playing a game with myself, effortlessly lobbing casts to likely looking bass lairs, seeing how closely I could place the lure and gloating over those places I correctly guessed held fish.

At last, when the sun dropped behind the fringed forest edge on the far end of Crooked Lake, I retrieved my last cast and stowed the rod. There was no sound in the night, not even a loon, and even the breeze had died completely. I could hear only the gentle lapping of the water on the quiet canvas skin of the canoe and Gypsy's soft breathing. I turned in the canoe to the east. Already a few bright stars glimmered in the eastern sky. Back to the west the sun was completely gone, having rolled up for the night the carpet of flame it had spread upon the water. The sky, however, was an unbroken band of orange, as if the entire world beyond Crooked Lake was aflame. Where the flames died out into the darkness of night the few clouds were lit from below and glowed purple and gray.

I had been wrong. It was not a nearly perfect night. It was perfect. Nothing, not even the horrendous flies during the day, yesterday's difficult paddle and the dirty campsite could taint this evening. Chilled, I picked up the paddle, gave the sunset one more longing look and then turned the canoe east to camp. Mary Jo had a fire going. There was time yet for a brandy before bed.

I knew then that no matter what we would encounter in our official duties this summer we were being paid amply for our time here.

Awoke to ominous clouds and rumbling thunder. Called Ely and received a sunny, 90 degree forecast. Hah! Within minutes it was pouring with both violent thunder and lightning, pinning us in the tent until afternoon. Discovered that, unfortunately, our USFS tent leaks.

After the rain we managed to complete campsite clean-up work in the area, although high winds prevented very much traveling.

◆ AT HOME IN THE WOODS ◆

Even as I lay there in a half awake stupor, I could sense the approaching storm. Though barely audible, the deep rumbling of the thunder sent tremors through the earth, ancient precambrian rock vibrating to the force they had weathered for eons. Not exactly the kind of morning I had hoped for.

I unzipped the window at the back of the tent. To the west I could see thunderheads piling up in black pyramids, marching down Sunday Bay. The sky above us was still blue, but that obviously would not last long. When I triggered the two-way radio, it snapped with the crackle of the air's electricity. I called Ely.

Though we were only twenty-five miles to the north, we might as well have been on another continent. The dispatcher gave me a sunny, ninety degree forecast and I chuckled as I listened. I relayed the coming of the storm to headquarters and suggested they might want to inform other crews on the border what may be coming their way. It looked to be a particularly violent tempest.

No sooner had I cleared the airwaves when the tent began to shake. Strong winds whipped violently at the tent fly, rattling it like a limp sail. Within seconds the first drops splattered on the roof, at first sounding like a succession of wet snowballs, so large were they. Then came a staccato drumming, the intervals between drops shortening, ending with the all-over wet of a steady, hard rain. It looked as though we wouldn't be going anywhere for awhile.

I lay back in my bag, staring at the roof, listening to the rain. Just as I was starting to fall back to sleep, a cold drop of water landed on my right eye. Great, our USFS tent leaked. I scooted to one side and put a towel on the floor beneath the steady drip.

The whole of the air seemed alive with wind, rain and thunder. The crashes grew more frequent and intense until at one point I flinched as one ripped loose directly overhead. The tent was flapping madly, the wind roaring through the jack pines above the tent and thunder filled our ears. Gypsy lay curled in a ball in one corner of the tent, her ears drawn back in fright, her whole body trembling.

"Are we going to be OK?" asked Mary Jo. Only her mouth, nose and eyes could be seen poking from the top of her bag.

"Don't worry Hon. There aren't any big pines near us so we shouldn't have to worry about lightning strikes. If we don't drown in this leaky tent, we'll be fine."

I wished I honestly believed what I was saying. Ever since Mary Jo and I spent a similar, terrifying morning in a tent on Metacryst Lake, far off the beaten track in the Quetico, I had worried about such storms. Stupidly we had pitched our tent beneath an enormous white pine and when the storm hit just as we were rising, I could only think of those wonderful electrical conductors, known as roots, that snaked their way beneath our tent. If lightning struck the pine it would flash through the trunk, down the roots, and right into our tent. This is not a needless fear for almost every year someone is killed in the canoe country by such lightning strikes. I tried to reassure myself, as I had Mary Jo, that the trees surrounding us were too small to warrant the lightning's attention.

If you believe that man is such a magnificent character, that he is so powerful and indomitable, try lying in a tent during a wilderness thunderstorm. You will quickly realize just how puny you are. It is a sobering experience.

66

The good side to such storms is that, if you have the nerves for it, you can grab a couple of hours of extra sleep. You might also read a book, if you had the foresight to pack one along. Should you neither be able to read, or sleep, you can always ponder life's intricate mysteries. With Mary Jo back sleeping, and Gypsy trembling, I had the time to contemplate our experiences to date.

There comes a time when you finally feel comfortable in a more primitive surrounding, even with a thunderstorm raging about you, a time when any perceived discomforts become the norm and are therefore hardly noticed. Thirteen days into our summer long adventure, I was suddenly aware that I had not given the outside world much thought for some time. I had not thought about whether or not our house was still standing or if business calls were piling up back in Duluth. The routine of hauling water from the lake or river, baking in our little folding oven or cooking over a campfire, watching sunsets over dark spruce forests and paying strict attention to the weather had become ingrained. Life became simple. All other existence seemed to have dissolved away.

And why not? We are reasonably well fed, reasonably clean and reasonably housed as opposed to being unreasonably over fed, unreasonably (almost fetishly) clean and unreasonably too well housed as is the norm in our society. Since we are incumbered with few possessions here, our simple little cabin houses not only ourselves comfortably but all that we own. It is not so back home where every nook and cranny seems to fill with the bulk of consumerism. I haven't thought about buying anything for days.

What, pray tell, would I buy? There is nothing out here that is not free for the asking. Can you buy a sunrise? Is there a price to the exhilaration we feel from the thunderstorm that rages outside? Nature is the truest democracy and not the richest man in the world is served a grander sunset than is the beggar.

No price tags hang in the forest. I asked a spider if he would weave me a web and found he had done so for free, not only constructing one but had it bejeweled with dawn's fresh dew, lit by the rising sun. When the breeze quaked his web, his jewels dripped to the earth by the dozen but the spider did not weep. The next morning he would be wealthy again. And so would we.

We eat simply, or simply eat, not to entertain or pass the time but to fuel our bodies. The work we do is sometimes hard but not difficult. Our muscles have responded and the joy of physical labor has replaced the early aches and pains. We paddle without thinking, almost as if we were breathing. Pure water has flushed our systems clean and no drink has ever tasted so fine as a draft of river water. We can fill our mug for free and there is no bartender to tip.

We need to heed no clothing fashion. We dress to suit our wants and the only critic we encounter is the mosquito, and if our clothing does not please him, if he gets his nose bent out of joint when testing it, then the style suits us all the better.

The cabin stays cool on the hottest day and is tight against the rains, unlike our tent. There are visitors enough, small brown ones with big soft ears, but even they have learned not to wear out their welcome. We could seat a thousand of them, and probably have. Wild flowers bloom in profusion out each door.

We hear no news of the outside world, nor do we ask. The center of our world is here and unless the news involves wind, rain or fire, it is unimportant. Will the seas be big tomorrow? Will the thunderstorms let up? Could we be so lucky as to have a tail wind?

These are as difficult as most questions here get. I wish only that it could stay that way always.

My feet suddenly felt wet. I looked at my sleeping bag and saw that the end was soaked. Wonderful. A leak at both ends of the tent. I scrunched up into a fetal position. The storm raged on. Mary Jo slept. Gypsy quivered.

I could add one more to my list of not-so-difficult questions. Did all Forest Service tents leak, or were we the only lucky ones? I dug out a battered paperback and turned to Twain for a little levity.

Left Saturday Bay at 8:40 am. Stopped at site #8, Friday Bay. Found much garbage and one hundred and thirteen fish carcasses left in campsite (44 walleyes, 51 smallmouth and 18 northern pike).
Cleaned campsite. Raced thunderstorm to cabin.

·ANNIVERSARY·

I awoke early. The tan roof of the tent was spread limply above my head, no whisper of a wind to stir it. I always hope to see the tent lit brightly from without, the portent of a sunny day, but this morning the nylon was drab, even though we faced east. On one elbow I peered out the mesh window. The day was calm and overcast, the sky a great gray sheet of dirty fabric.

Gypsy looked up at me as I stirred, opening her eyes but not lifting her head. As she grows older she is not so anxious to jump up and head outside, satisfied to stay curled in a tight, sleepy ball until she sees I am ready to leave the tent.

Mary Jo slept soundly still. We have had no problem with sleep this summer, for the most part finding ourselves seeking the sleeping bag even before the long summer days have ended. Morning comes early as well and though we are amply rewarded with the canoe country's rich beauty day in and day out, the one gift we have not been given is the luxury of sleeping in. Jerry Jussila and the two-way radio make sure of that.

Silently I slipped into my clothes, laced up my boots and headed outside, leaving Mary Jo to slumber awhile longer. Gypsy scooted out the door as soon as it was unzipped, pausing to stretch luxuriously as soon as she was in the open. I too arched my back, forcing the kinks from my neck and shoulders.

Crooked Lake lay silver gray, the water appearing almost thick as it heaved slowly with the rhythm of breath. I put a match to the kindling in the firegrate, watched the yellow flames spurt up through the bark and tinder, placed a couple of small sticks into the gathering tongues and walked to the water's edge with our blackened coffee pot.

The water that had appeared heavy as oil a few seconds before swam clearly into the pot as I eased it into the lake, breaking the surface tension. With the pot almost full I walked back up to the fire, wet hands feeling the water's coolness. A few minutes later, after lowering the food pack and digging out the makings for breakfast, I dumped one, two, three tablespoons of coffee into the cold water and placed it on the fire to boil. Gypsy was drinking at the lake.

I quietly entered the tent, kicked the pine needles from my boots and opened my camera bag. Fumbling in its depths I found a battered envelope, extracted it and crawled over to Mary Jo.

"Wake up, Hon. Happy Anniversary! Coffee's on."

Mary Jo opened her eyes, smiled at me and sat up. I handed the card to her.

"What's this?"

"Didn't think I'd remember, huh?" I laughed. "It's an anniversary card. Go ahead. Open it up."

"Have you been carrying this with you the whole time?" she asked, tearing the envelope open. She read the card and smiled again.

"Yup. Happy anniversary!" I replied as we embraced. "Coffee's going and I'll start breakfast while you dress. We should get an early start. I think it might rain today."

Breakfast done, camp broke and the canoe loaded, we pushed off onto the still calm waters of Crooked. Overhead the grayness had not abated but a slight stirring of the air foretold a change in the weather. With the coming of the breeze the hordes of nasty flies that had tortured us the last few days were shaken from their hiding places and as we wound our way east through the channels of Crooked Lake, they descended upon our canoe. I had the sinking feeling that this was not going to be the most pleasant day we had ever spent in the canoe country.

Our first stop was at an island campsite at the north end of Friday Bay. Although we had been told of the enormous amount of dead fish found here by a group of passing canoeists some days earlier, nothing could have prepared us for what we found, nor were the warnings even necessary for as we neared the site the stench of dead fish wafted across the water, alerting us to what we would find. When we landed a black cloud of flies lifted from the grisly scene.

Scattered across what normally would have been a clean shelf of Canadian Shield granite were the horrid remains of some destructive group's wanton act. Filleted bass, walleye and northern pike were lying everywhere and bloated, uncleaned carcasses bobbed sickly in the water along shore. Huge amounts of garbage were also strewn about the campsite, including discarded, soiled clothing, food, books and magazines and a pile of plywood and PVC pipe that evidently joined together to form a picnic table. Even worse, they had shit on the tent sites.

We turned to the noisome task of cleaning the mess. The rains that had kept us in our tent yesterday had soaked the filth, making the task even more unpleasant. Gypsy scurried into the undergrowth of cedars in an effort to escape the almost unbearable flies. We built a huge, cleansing fire in the grate and burned what we could and put the nonburnables into the canoe. While the putrid piles burned we picked up the fish remains, which totaled one hundred and thirteen, and hauled them back into the woods to be buried. While I buried the fish, Mary Jo had the nasty job of disposing of the human waste left for us by this group of cretins. We were both much angered and saddened by what we saw.

We couldn't leave the campsite fast enough. The sky had grown darker and while I did not wish to be drenched by rain, I thought that a good washing of this site by a storm might by just the thing it needed to erase the stench, the only tangible sign left after our cleaning. We put the fire out, slid our canoe into the lake and piled in, tired, angry and dirty. Maybe a rain would do us good too.

It is one thing to contemplate a cleansing downpour and another to actually sit in one. We stroked our way through the humid day across the confluence of Friday and Thursday Bays, up through the spruce bound narrows of the Big Current and headed south on the last leg back to the cabin. No matter how hard or fast we paddled we could not shed the veil of flies shrouded over our canoe and Gypsy lay irritated in the bow, snapping at her miserable tormentors.

As we turned east around Pancake Point in Wednesday Bay I looked over my shoulder to the north and west. Thunderheads piled ominously behind us, white crests giving way to gray bellies and black trunks, the whole mass leaning over as if to engulf us. Wet skirts dragged along the horizon. It was raining hard to the west. Our camp of last night was probably already soaked by the storm. Soon the water would flush the fish camp in Friday Bay.

With that sight we decided that we would rather be bathed in hot water back at the cabin than by a driving rain and dug diligently into the dark waters. A wind had come up and fortunately it was at our backs, helping us in our race with the storm. We shot through the shallow bay, past historic Table Rock campsite and turned to the south. There would be no time to fish the currents of Smallmouth Rapids and we powered through its ripples and toward the Pictured Rocks.

We stopped for a breather beneath the weathered cliffs and gazed absently at the pictographs. They seemed sullen this day, ominous, and the misshepezhieu coiled its serpent tail and stared back at us with its horned head. It seemed a warning to stay off the water and I glanced one last time at the approaching storm. It was raining in Wednesday Bay. The atmosphere shuddered with thunder. The air about us grew heavy and calm and the flies in the canoe went crazy with activity. We had better hurry if we were going to win our race with the thunderstorm.

Now the waters broke thickly on our bow, parting in soft folds as we gathered momentum. Nothing was stirring except our flies. The lake lay flat. I could feel the storm slanting over me, hear its rumbling breath. If there was to be lightning we had best make land soon.

The falls came into view. Smoke from the campsite at its feet drifted parallel to the water, snaking horizontally into the cabin bay. We shot through the narrow gap behind the island at its mouth and paddled furiously to the boathouse. In only minutes we had tossed our tools and gear into the boathouse, rolled the canoe up alongside its protective walls and found ourselves racing up the trail to the cabin. A drop of water that felt the size of an egg splattered on the back of my neck as we reached the cabin door. We had won the race.

Inside the cabin we watched as the storm flew down the lake, whipping the tree tops and stirring the waters. Soon the windows were streaming, even protected under the eaves, the water blown sideways by the gale. Thunder clapped overhead and Gypsy slunk into the bedroom and hid. Never had the cabin felt so welcome.

We settled down. Mary Jo retrieved a snack from a food pack and I poured us each a shot of brandy.

"Happy anniversary, Mary Jo," I said wearily.

"Happy anniversary, Michael," she answered as we clicked our plastic camp cups together in a toast.

"Hell of a way to spend it, though," she added.

Received a visit at 10:00 a.m. from Minnesota Department of Natural Resources Conservation Officer Art Gensmer and pilot Dan Ross. They flew in to get the particulars about the fish incident in Friday Bay. We gave them the details and they left to inspect the site.

We rescued a "misplaced" USFS firegrate from a campsite in the Quetico, Moose Bay. Returned it to campsite #33.

◆ HOW TO INSTALL A USFS FIREGRATE ◆

The night had been cool. Billowing white clouds floated serenely in the blue morning sky, punctuated occasionally by a few dark, dirty ones. While I pride myself on being somewhat adept at reading weather I never know what this phenomenon means. Were these dark clouds sprinkled amongst the white an omen of bad weather to come, or were they merely left over from some system that had passed this way while we slept? The day would tell the story.

Being a Saturday we received our morning radio call from Voyageur Visitor Center rather than Headquarters. I enjoy listening to the morning call for not only are we contacted but so are all other crews in the field. Sometimes we can only hear the call from Ely and not the field crews' reply and so we get some interesting half conversations, our imaginations actively trying to fill in the gaps. Usually it is Jerry Jussila we hear as he contacts each group in turn. We might hear him talk to a crew at Kekakabic Lake, another on Lake Four or even a chat with Dorothy Molter to our east on Knife Lake. When the reception is good it is not unusual for us to hear the Cook District contact their wilderness rangers on sprawling Lac La Croix. It is a little like being an eavesdropper. It also makes us feel as though we are part of a very important team.

While I do not always agree with Forest Service policies or their priorities, I have nothing but admiration for those rangers we have met. Theirs is a difficult and often frustrating job, as we have found, and they do this job well. They are not rewarded with great wealth or fame but with the knowledge that they are guarding a most precious resource and I have felt their love for the canoe country. Most of these men and women are quiet but in their eyes is the gleem of the adventurer. Being a part of this team, even for just one summer, and "honorary" members at that, is a thrill.

The first task each day that we are at the cabin is to check our trapline. Gathering up the traps, Gypsy escorts me to the mouse burial grounds out the back door. There is always a pang of guilt in this job, especially if I look closely at the deer mice, for they can be described in no better way than cute. Food out here is a precious resource though, particularly when I recall lugging it all in on our backs, and we can not afford to share it with mice.

While I was conducting this burial service I heard Mary Jo answer a call on the radio. Returning to the cabin I found out we were expecting an unusual visit, especially so because our guests were flying in. There is an air ban on the BWCAW and only officials of the Forest Service or Minnesota Department of Natural Resources are allowed to land airplanes within the wilderness, and then only for important purposes. I scanned the sky from the back door.

The radio began to crackle again. "Crooked Lake, Crooked Lake, what is your location?"

Hustling to the microphone I responded quickly.

"We are at the cabin, at Lower Basswood Falls."

"We'll be there in five minutes," came the reply.

That was the end of the transmission. Mary Jo and I were still guessing who it was we had talked to, or why, when the drone of a small airplane passed over the cabin. We raced down the trail to the boathouse.

The pilot skillfully maneuvered the plane into a line down the narrow channel heading toward Crooked Lake and brought it gently down with hardly more wake than a small boat would make. Taxiing the single engine plane through the maze of islands and reefs below the falls took equal skill and we both watched in anticipation, waiting on the dock to lash the floats in place. As they neared I could see two men inside and the insignia of the Minnesota DNR on their caps and guessed they must be Conservation Officers. That's game warden in common parlance.

Art Gensmer and the pilot, Dan Ross, stepped from the plane and shook our hands soundly. Both were big men. Any violator stopped by either of these wardens would surely note their size and would think twice before giving them grief. I know I would have. I felt like a munchkin in their presence.

In anticipation of their arrival we had put on a fresh pot of coffee. This was a novelty for us, to actually have someone check out one of our complaints regarding a violation and I was happy that the information we had radioed to Ely regarding the fish camp had found its way to the proper authorities. Management of most game and fish within the BWCAW, including the laws regulating harvest, falls under the Minnesota DNR even though the area is a federally protected wilderness. I'm sure they sensed, sitting at our little table over a cup of coffee, our anger and dismay as we relayed the details of our discovery in Friday Bay. They sat quietly as we rambled, Art taking notes on a small pad. Both asked us a few pertinent questions and we replied as thoroughly as we could.

When the coffee was gone and the questions answered we escorted the two wardens to our little dock and saw them off. With the roar of the engine echoing off the spruce clad hills, the plane jumped nimbly from the water and was quickly gone to the north. Reaching Friday Bay takes us hours by canoe. No doubt they were landing at the campsite by the time we reached the cabin.

Today we had an unusual task. Jerry Jussila had informed us yesterday that a Forest Service firegrate had been found in the Quetico, in a campsite in Moose Bay. Located a half mile northeast of the Pictured Rocks, Moose Bay is the estuary to the Tuck River which flows from clear Robinson Lake. Hardly able to believe someone would steal a fifty pound iron firegrate and remove it to another campsite, our job was to locate it and install it in the site from which it had disappeared.

We had made an attempt yesterday to do just that but had been waylaid by the discovery of a family camped illegally on the U.S portage of Lower Basswood Falls. By time we had found the family, for the camp was deserted except for an unattended campfire when we spotted it, the day was growing late. We gave them a hand in moving to an unoccupied designated campsite and parted on friendly terms. Their teenage daughter looked so embarrassed because her father had not only instructed them to camp illegally but had brought them in the day later than their permit specified, it was hard to get angry. After escorting them to a campsite we spent the rest of the day trying to make this spot on the portage *not* look like a campsite. It is a problem area for many choose to ignore the rules and camp there anyway.

With the Canadian authorities permission to land on their soil (our summer permit allowed us only to stray into Canadian waters) we started to search for the firegrate. On a point of land near the entrance to Moose Bay we found the grate standing forlornly above a bed of dead coals. Trying to carry it down to our canoe I hypothesized that whoever had stolen this grate not only had a strong back but a very weak mind. It weighed a ton.

Moose Bay is a miraculous bit of water. Once you paddle over the sand bar at the bay's entrance you can not help but be taken by the clarity of the water. While the water of the Basswood River and Crooked Lake is clean, it is bog stained and appears to be the color of tea. Not so in Moose Bay where the water flows clear as it heads south to mingle with the darker waters of Crooked Lake. Taking the opportunity to paddle north to where the Tuck River enters the bay we were amazed to be able to peer down and see many large fish swimming near the bottom. Since we had brought our water bag with to fill and return to the cabin, we decided that a different flavor might be in order for a change, the flavor of Moose Bay. We filled the bag and all our water bottles happily with the clear fluid before searching for the firegrate's original campsite.

Their are two U.S. campsites near Moose Bay and we guessed that no matter how weak a mind the firegrate thieves had, they likely would not have gone far after stealing the grate. The second site we checked, the first one north of the pictographs, revealed a large hole in the ground from which the grate had been wrestled. We had solved the case of the missing firegrate.

The only question now was what to do with the grate. In the map case we had a small book, a bible of sorts for wilderness rangers. In it the Forest Service sets out very definite criteria for how each job should be done, from the width of portage trails to the installation of latrines. I dug the book out and paged through it. On page sixty-five I found the instructions we needed under the heading of "Proper Installation of the F.S. Fire Grate." There would be no question now on just how to secure the grate.

For all of you have have paddled the BWCAW and ever wondered how those firegrates are installed, pay attention. What you see above ground is only about half of the grate. Except for those that are anchored in rock (which is done by drilling holes with a hand hammer drill), a trench five feet long by sixteen inches wide by one foot deep is specified. The grate is leveled in the bottom of the hole and at least three logs not less that three inches in diameter and longer than the grate are placed across the bottom cross members, down the length of the grate. On top of these logs large rocks are placed to further anchor the arrangement. Finally the rest of the hole is filled with smaller rocks and mineral soil to provide a surface through which the fire will not burn and then three sides of the grate are built up with the ever present rock windscreen.

Which is exactly what Mary Jo and I did, leaving a perfectly level grate with a beautifully constructed windscreen (well, as perfect as you can get using a water bottle as a carpenter's level) for the next campers.

By the time we were done I had some serious questions about the sanity of whoever had removed the grate. While the job we had just completed was not overly difficult, we had all the proper tools, including a shovel. Taking the grate from this site would have required an equal amount of labor, or maybe more without tools. Why anyone would have bothered was beyond me.

In any case, the grate had been returned and installed. We stood back and admired our handiwork. Our clothing and hands were black and our faces streaked from handling the sooty grate but we were pleased. It looked to us to be a job well done and if I had been installing a new grate, I would have said it would also be permanent. Knowing the history of this grate, however, I had some doubts as to how long it would stay there.

Awoke to the sound of an outboard motor at 6:10 am. By time I could get outside it had passed toward Wednesday Bay.

Paddled to Wednesday Bay and interviewed all campers to get description of motor ban violators. Checked all campsites and latrines for needed work, gave sites 28 through 32 a thorough cleaning. Found ten pounds of pickling salt at Table Rock campsite.

Were nearly run down by motorized canoe as we returned to cabin, near site #33, 6:40 p.m. Description as follows:

Square stern, olive drab aluminum canoe, camouflaged motor, three adults, two in camouflage, one in black and white plaid wool shirt. The one in the plaid shirt was possibly a woman, sandy hair. One man had a black beard. Both men had hoods on and hid their faces as they passed. Faint numbers on canoe bow, could only read MN 69???X. Shot about ten frames of film of them as they passed by.

• ILLUSION •

I thought I was having a bad dream. Deep in sleep I struggled with the sound of a motor, something we had not heard for some time, convinced in my sleepy stupor I was only dreaming. Something, however, brought me to the surface, as if pulling me up out of a deep hole, and when I shook the sleep from my mind I realized I was not imagining things. I was hearing an outboard motor.

I quickly shouted Mary Jo awake. "There's a goddamn motor outside, Hon. Wake up. I'm going to the lake to see what's going on."

As fast as I could I threw on some clothes and my moccasins and raced down the trail to the lake shore. By the time I reached the water the motorized craft could not be seen but its droning burned through the morning calm. I stood as still as I could to listen. The sound was disappearing toward Wednesday Bay. Long after it actually was beyond hearing, I could yet hear it in my mind, a swath of noise cut through the silence of my subconscious. It pestered me, like the incessant buzz of a mosquito in a tent at night.

I was really pissed off.

After eating breakfast and packing a lunch and tools, Mary Jo, Gypsy and I paddled to Wednesday Bay. While there was no way we could ever hope to catch up to a motor powered canoe, I did hope that we would be able to interview some canoeists who may have gotten a better view than I had. A good description would be helpful in the event the Forest Service decided to pursue this matter.

What we did find was a lot of angry folks. A few offered descriptions and most concurred: three adults in an 18 foot square stern aluminum canoe, either olive drab in color or camouflaged, as was the motor.

This, however, was not what most wanted to talk about. They were dismayed and angry, angry that these three had utterly ruined their wilderness canoe trip. I felt relieved that my anger was not unfounded, that others shared my sense of dismay.

Wilderness is, after all, an illusion in today's world. Few places are de facto wilderness anymore, wilderness in the sense they are impenetrable. Most, especially in the lower forty-eight states, are wilderness only in that they have been protected by law, that restrictions have been placed on numbers of people permitted to enter and the modes of travel allowed within. The Quetico-Superior canoe country is actually much larger than the areas set aside within the BWCAW and Quetico Provincial Park. Similar country with miles of canoe routes lie outside the official boundaries but are no longer wilderness, crisscrossed with logging roads and highways and dotted with resorts and summer cottages. The wilderness canoe country has shrunk to those sections within the imaginary borders of the BWCAW and Quetico and is only wilderness because the laws keep it so. Apparently this designation was not so sanctified as we had been led to believe.

Those who had entered the wilderness by motor broke not only the law, but the spell of wilderness. They are criminals as surely as a bank robber for they stole something even more valuable than money. What did these three steal? From the time they passed from the area in which motors are allowed into the non-motorized section they went by nearly fifty campsites. Within most of those campsites were parties who had obeyed the law, had paddled into the wilderness to seek its silence. These are people who, for a variety of reasons, had sought out this tranquility, who had perhaps saved a week's valuable vacation time to renew their spirits in the bosom of solitude. If there were four people per party, and most campsites were occupied, it is possible that in the span of one or two hours these camouflaged clowns had disrupted the trips of almost two hundred people.

That is what they stole. Two hundred vacations, the solitude yearned for by hundreds of noise and city weary campers. What value can you put on the months of planning, the weeks of working, the pigeon-holed vacation days spent by those who managed to find a quiet bit of wilderness to call their own for a few days? And in a flash, the illusion was shattered, the remoteness of muscle powered travel rung hollow by the immediacy of motors.

Which is what I sensed in, or was said by, all those we spoke to this day. Anger flashed in nearly every eye. They felt violated, as surely as if some burglar had entered their home and stolen their most valuable possessions. A stolen stereo could be replaced. How do you restore the illusion of wilderness, how do you keep it from tainting the rest of your trip, or even future trips, once it is gone?

This evening, as Mary Jo and I returned to the cabin, I halted the canoe just north of the pictographs. We floated between the mainland and a narrow island at the mouth of Moose Bay. I was beginning to think this event had worn down my nerves for I could still hear the sound of motors. My imagination must have gotten the best of me.

Then I realized that I was not hearing things. The sound of a motor penetrated the evening air and it grew louder as it neared. Quickly I scrambled to put a long lens on my camera. Although we had no law enforcement powers, and could expect no assistance from Ely, I would at least try to photograph these morons as they motored by. We sat and waited.

They came around the bend from the north and swung passed us. Two were in camouflage clothing and one in a plaid shirt, this one possibly a woman or maybe a slightly built young man. When they saw us they neither veered or slowed down but motored on by, the two men shielding their faces with their hands, like criminals being hauled into a police station hounded by television cameras.

The motor drive on my camera whirred. I shot ten quick frames and then they were gone, down past the pictographs and toward the falls. Their wake lapped noisily on the shore and tossed the canoe about as we sat in disbelief. It was ironic that the little island to our left that still rung with the sound of motors was the same one that Sigurd Olson had come to and written about because of the profound sense of silence he had found there.

I felt emasculated. There had been nothing we could do but what we had. Perhaps the photos might lead to an arrest, but I had my doubts. The Forest Service was so understaffed that such things had a low priority. I questioned those priorities. Which is more important, a well brushed portage trail or protecting the essence of wilderness? Where best could their budget-crunched manpower and resources be spent? Which is more likely to ruin a canoe trip, an unkempt portage or a campsite full of garbage and decaying fish, motors buzzing nearby? If those bent on breaking the law knew just how few and far between real rangers actually were, if they knew that Mary Jo and I were the only Forest Service presence in the over thirty water miles distance between Basswood and Curtain Falls, they would probably be in here more frequently. And since we were the only rangers, volunteer or otherwise, to patrol Crooked Lake, I took their insult personally.

Stayed near the cabin as Mary Jo is not feeling well. Cleaned Basswood River campsites #17 and #19. Latrine at #18 is old, broken and full. Will replace it soon. #19 has a new style latrine with a DEEP hole. Whoever dug it must have needed a ladder to climb out.

Took the opportunity to do a bit of exploring on this fine, sunny day, poking into some out of the way corners of our territory nearby.

Saw a whitetail doe today.

◆ THE LITTLE CREEK ◆

I don't know why I steered the canoe into the hidden bay. In fact, before we rounded the last bend past a campsite on a small, piney point, I wasn't sure there was even water beyond. Such was our pace this day that we were willing to let the wanderlust take over, wanting to spend time to find places that, though near the main travel routes, were not visited frequently. Few are the times in nature that leisure can not be afforded.

Once we entered the bay, water lilies beginning to bloom along the south bank, I knew why I had been drawn to this spot. Here was a quiet little corner of the world where one could easily imagine that nothing else existed. Far horizons and great vistas are often inspiring and beautiful but for me it is always the intimate niches that capture my attention. This was a perfect place, a quiet place complete with water, pines, blooming flowers and a campsite. It was a spot one could get to know.

As perfect as was this bay, it was the little creek that must have drawn us here. We had not been aware of its gay song until we rounded the point, but there could be no mistaking the gurgle and hiss of it

as it poured into the east end of the bay. A small cataract, so very different than that of churning Lower Basswood Falls a mile away, tumbled privately across round rocks, feeding its water into that of the mighty Basswood River. It had no delusions as to its grandeur, hiding shyly under an arch of trees.

Flowing water draws not only me, but many people, and this time was no exception. The bank was muddy near the creek, a thick stand of horsetail growing to the right. We paddled hard to get the canoe as far up onto the soft bank as we could and then stepped out into the pungent muck. Gypsy leaped gracefully from the bow to shore, never muddying her paws.

I had wondered about this spot and whether we would find a portage here. Though the chain of lakes is small, it showed clearly on the map and I have found from long years of canoe travel that where there are lakes in close proximity to each other, inevitably you will find a portage. If there is a creek connecting two lakes, it is usually a good place to look for a portage. The low places through which they flow are natural spots for level portages.

Although there was little evidence of frequent use, there indeed was a portage here and it matched the scale of the creek and bay. Canopied, it wandered up a slight incline, twisting around deadfalls but always within earshot, if not sight, of the creek. When it topped the last rise, perhaps only twenty rods from our canoe, it dropped four or five feet into the shallow, log choked end of a pretty little lake.

Gypsy and I were first across the portage and when we reached the end, I abruptly grabbed her collar. She gave me a startled look for she had neither leash nor lead on her since we had left Ely and no doubt she was confused. A breeze blew in off the lake and she instantly became rigid, ears up and nose working. Mary Jo came up from behind and I whispered "sit" to all. We hid behind the upthrust roots of a fallen spruce.

In front of us, not thirty feet away, standing elegantly on a crossing of fallen logs, was a whitetail deer. A sleek doe, she was in the summer red pelage that is so striking. Her every move poured grace. Once or twice she stopped to nibble at small plants that grew from the duff caught in the logs and then she stepped into the shallow water to take a drink. Her ears and tail were twitching but not in fright at our presence for I was convinced she did not know we were admiring her. Flies buzzed about her head and hind quarters and the constant flicking of appendages at both ends was to ward off the pesky insects.

The red deer, the perfect blue of the lake stretching out behind her, the dark spruce of the forest and the pure green of grass and arrowhead made a picture and frame so gorgeous as to cause me to let an audible sigh. Mary Jo and I looked at each other and smiled. This was the reward we had come to this country for.

Perhaps it was my sigh that alerted the deer. She suddenly became rigid and we could see the tensing of her muscles. Since we were downwind, she had no sure idea of whether something was really watching her but she did not waste time. Two or three leisurely steps, as if to pretend she was in no hurry, then a quick bound and she vanished behind the screen of forest. We heard her stop a few yards into the heavy cover long enough to bawl us out with that surprisingly mule-like bray of the whitetail doe.

When she was gone the scene, though still beautiful, was somehow empty.

I looked down at Gypsy. She too was tensed, every muscle rock hard, the flame of her wild brethren green in her eyes. Like us, the primitive in her is just below the surface although it would be much easier for her to slip into those wild ways than it would for most of us. I calmly told her "no" and she knew what it meant, that she could not chase after the deer. Her wild chases would have to be confined to deer mice, not deer, and there would be no exciting pursuit through the forest, but instead through the legs of table and chairs in the dark cabin at night. She turned with me to walk back down the portage for, while she is a very good dog, she is not beyond temptation, and I decided to distance her from the still hot track of the deer.

Now this was a portage! Twisting, thick, still with soil and plants underfoot. It had not been trodden to mud under the weight of weary campers. There showed no treads of Nikes and Reeboks here. The trail flowed, like the creek, around or over obstructions. It had likely changed course before, and would again, as windstorms and old age caused deadfalls to block the passage. There were no canoe rests, no footprints, no litter and it was just wide enough to let a person through with a canoe on their back, and no more. This was my kind of portage.

Before we launched the canoe we took a walk to where the little creek met the bay. The water was so clear that if it had not been moving, rippling in the sunlight, one could deceive himself that it really wasn't there. Strands of grassy water plants clung to the bottom and waved as if in a wind, bowing downstream. Wherever it passed over a rock the clear waters boiled white as air was churned into it, bubbles trailing into the bay to pop one at a time.

Upstream it passed over a series of steps, one tiny waterfall after the next, each one slightly larger as they progressed downstream. The creek flowed out of a dark green tunnel of alder, arching entirely over the water. I sat on my haunches on a rock midstream and looked up under the meshing limbs, seeing white waters tumble over black rock amidst the dancing shadows of leaves.

The water looked so fine I had to take a drink. Cool, it quenched my thirst and buoyed my spirit. The water washing over the toes of my boots hurried busily into the bay, into the main river and down to Crooked Lake. From there it would flow west to the Rainy River country and then north towards Lake Winnipeg. Undaunted, the water from this little creek, mingled with that of countless others like it, would turn easterly and with a last push through high, clay banks, mix with the salt water of Hudson's Bay. Today smallmouth bass found it home. Someday, maybe, it would caress beluga whales. I toasted it on its journey with another drink.

All the water that has ever been, or ever will be, is here now. It sits, it runs, it rises as mist. It evaporates and falls again as rain or snow. The canoe country is rich in water and far removed from civilization yet in the clear, deep lakes traces of pesticides and heavy metals reside, deposited there from the dirty outside world through the air and in the otherwise life giving rains and snow. You cannot pollute a drop of water anywhere without it eventually poisoning some distant place.

The public seems satisfied with setting aside a few wild places, like the BWCAW. Setting wilderness aside is only one equation in the formula for a healthy planet. More important is setting aside the excesses in lifestyle. The world can not operate with only a few pieces of the ecosystem functioning.

The sun was westering. This had been an easy, happy day, highlighted by our visit to the little creek and the whitetail doe. Since we were done cleaning campsites for the day, and Mary Jo had a hankering for a fresh fish dinner (when doesn't she!), we decided to fish our way back to the cabin.

I pushed the canoe out of the muck and into the hidden bay. The clear water of the creek gave way to the dark waters of the Basswood River as we pointed the canoe through the narrows and into the expanse beyond. A fresh breeze greeted us from the north to make our paddle home easier. Our rods are always rigged up in the hope that we might be able to sneak a few minutes fishing into our day. I passed Mary Jo's to her and while I was still retrieving mine, she hooked into a smallmouth bass. Mary Jo gives a fish no quarter, leaning into the battle with all her might. The bass dived deeply, swapped ends, rocketed to the surface and flashed brilliantly in the low, late sun, the spray of its leap a glistening fountain. Soon it tired and Mary Jo eased it to the canoe, pinching the bass's lower lip between her thumb and forefinger. She hoisted it up for me to see, a smile splitting her face. It was a nice size bass. It was also, unfortunately for it, just the right size for dinner. I passed the stringer to Mary Jo.

We kept fishing just for the sheer pleasure of it, letting the wind carry us down the shore. I guided the canoe with a paddle, one handed, holding my fishing rod in the other. With my eyes closed I felt the warm sun on the back of my neck, heard the tinkle of our little creek behind the pine point in the secret bay. The waters are making their way to the north, I thought, the magical north, and to far off Hudson's Bay. The canoe country was weaving its intimate spell again, inviting me to explore deeper, to seek each creek's origin and the routes to hidden lakes. The call was strong, the urge intense.

A sharp rap on my lure jerked me from my thoughts and the spell faded slightly. There would be time some other day to let the call seduce me. Today there were fish to catch.

A long day. Paddled to Friday Bay and back today, cleaning twelve campsites. Most sites in good condition.

The eagles of Wednesday Bay showed off their young one today.

Found things, both strange and wonderful, in our travels today. We were also treated to yet another day of beautiful weather.

◆ SURPRISE FINDS ◆

We have come a long way, Mary Jo and I, both figuratively and physically. By my computations we paddled over twenty-five miles today in our circuitous, connect the dots (campsites) route, stopping to clean many campsites and do eagle surveys all the way from the cabin to Friday Bay and back.

Paddling has become so second nature that I was surprised to find we do not even stop to think about whether a distance is too great or our limbs are weary. Our soft city muscles have hardened to those of true voyageurs and the sheer exhilaration of our animal self is hard to now deny.

There were other surprises this day. One campsite we stopped at was so clean we both gasped a "wow" almost simultaneously. Not only had the occupants taken care to leave it in no worse shape than when they found it, they must have gone to pains to leave it better than when they had arrived. While the dogma of minimum impact camping dictates such behavior, we have not otherwise witnessed it to date. I would have liked to have met those campers and shook their hands.

There were some strange surprises as well. In one campsite we found a huge diving platform built well out over the waters of Friday Bay, constructed of a large felled tree, the lid from the latrine and many

boulders. The tree was anchored on a hillside with boulders built cairn-like over its base and was supported halfway along its length with a vertical member of log between it and the ground. The platform from which the divers must have launched themselves was the lid from the latrine, nailed to the end of the log. Ingenious, it must have taken hours to construct. It took hours to dismantle as well and we were careful to try and replace the boulders from the holes where they had formerly resided.

In yet another site we found a strange conglomeration of refuse. Stashed behind the latrine was a five gallon pail, a galvanized steel washtub and a thirty gallon plastic trash can! It would take a more twisted mind than mine to figure out why anyone would haul such things two days into the wilderness.

A pleasant surprise was the discovery that the eagles in Wednesday Bay have successfully reared one offspring. It tottered on the edge of the nest, its proud parents perched nearby, and flapped its wings in the strong breeze, testing itself and preparing for the not too distant day when it would soar for the first time.

Seeing the forest's young is always a great thrill and one that is usually rare. For good reason all animals keep their nearly helpless young well hidden and the fortunate voyageur who is treated to such a scene would do well to mark that day.

One great surprise find happened on an early lake trout fishing trip. It had been a late spring and the weather was still cool. Hardly a leaf had sprouted yet even though it was almost mid-May and the north woods looked more like November than it did spring. Still, one could sense the the sun that beat down was going to grow warmer, the days longer and that ever repeating ritual of rebirth was about to take place. Patches of snow clung in hollows on the north sides of the canoe country's hills. Mary Jo, Gypsy and I were drifting down the south shore of a small trout lake near Little Saganaga, tossing spoons and hooking the brilliant inland lake trout. Rounding a point we were both startled to see a disheveled cow moose standing in the forest, within ten feet of the lake.

She seemed unconcerned as we drifted ever nearer and I freed my camera from the day pack. The moose was black and grey and tan, the darker patches near her chest and legs, the lighter patches rising to her back and shoulders until she was topped with a buff colored saddle. Her winter coat was shedding in great, flapping hunks and the newer growth was almost fawn colored. She shook her mulish ears and watched us.

I had never seen a moose let us get as near to it as this one was and wondered if perhaps she might not be ill. Then when we were only a few feet from shore, not more than twenty feet from the cow, she backed up a few yards, keeping her chest toward us.

Mary Jo and I were whispering amazed comments to each other when I heard a sound.

"Hush! What's that?" I asked.

"Sounds like guinea pigs," Mary Jo said.

Guinea pigs? She was right. The thin, guttural squeakings we were hearing did sound like those made by a rodent. But where were they coming from?

Something moved where the cow moose had been standing. The moving thing squeaked. Another moving thing next to it squeaked in return. Then one of them stood.

Up from the grass came a calf moose, with wobbling legs, cocoa coat and wrinkled cauliflower ears. Its back legs gave way suddenly and it cried with fright. I quickly backed the canoe away so as to minimize our presence but there was no way now we could leave, caught by the spell of this wonderful sight. For a few moments it stood shakily and then trotted to its mother and crouched beneath her hulking body.

Its brother or sister still lay curled in a ball. With a lonesome wail it thrashed in the grass, finally finding itself standing on its stilt legs. Once up it wasted no time but fled the way of its sibling, its tiny black moose hooves flashing as it tottered away. With both calves safely with her the cow moved them just out of sight into the sparse spring undergrowth.

We had witnessed the first steps of new born moose.

Finally, the most beautiful surprise this day was the discovery of a stand of delicate violet irises. So intense was their hue that we spotted them from nearly one hundred yards away, growing precariously from a crack in bedrock near the water's edge. Their tenacity is to be admired for I can not imagine a less fertile spot in which to grow and yet there they were, nearly a dozen stalks two feet tall, each one waving proudly a banner of violet.

I mark this day as one where the balance of surprises was tipped in favor of the pleasant over the ugly or strange.

Put new style fiberglass latrine in site #17, Basswood River. Inspected other sites in the area and gave them a quick cleaning.

Lectured a group from a boys camp that were swimming at Lower Basswood Falls. Every time they would leap from the cliff into the water they would scream obscenities at the top of their lungs. Screaming in the wilderness is bad enough; those particular words were very inappropriate. The group leader did not think so and I can only describe him as a smart ass.

◆ LATRINES ◆

The first shovel full uproots small plants. Large leaf aster is most common but there are many others that fall victim to our shovel. When this sod is carefully cut away and set aside, to be used later to dress up the site, the earnest digging begins. If you are lucky there will be a few inches of real soil, loose and brown, that quickly is removed and piled to one side. By now the hole is two feet square and perhaps six to ten inches deep. Then the real work begins.

How many years of history one has cut through during this first step is hard to say. How long does it take to make an inch of top soil anywhere, let alone in the canoe country? That soil, comprised of decaying vegetable matter, which itself grows slowly here, certainly took centuries to accumulate. This area was stripped clean of any ancient soil by the passing of the glaciers ten thousand years ago. It is likely that these meager few inches of soil have taken that long to accumulate. Once you have gleefully cut through this soil (for there is pleasure in shoveling in soil that actually yields to the blade) comes the gravel, rock and clay.

The clay I believe is ancient sediment, formed when the lakes and rivers were higher, or perhaps siltation from glacial flow or from glacial lakes. We found it primarily along the Basswood River, often as far as one hundred yards from the present shoreline. It is grey and hard. Mary Jo says it is like trying to shovel frozen fudge. Each shovel-full sticks to the blade and a number of times we were nearly pulled over when trying to toss it. At this point work really slows down.

I find the clay most interesting. How long had it lay there, unexposed to the sun? For ten thousand years since the glaciers passed? Was this evidence of an ancient shoreline when the Basswood River was much higher, fiercer?

What would the river have looked like then? The falls would likely have been underwater but new ones would have existed where the channel went over what are now points or islands. Was there anyone here yet to see it? Had the Paleo-Indians followed the receding glaciers north this far by then? Were the early inhabitants hunting mastodon and musk ox? The canoe country would have been tundra then, at least for awhile. Or was this clay set down later, were there trees growing then, the black spruce, dwarf birch and willow that pressed north as the ice melted? It would have been a different place then, though the lakes and rivers were surely forming, filling and flowing with the melt water of the glaciers. Would it have looked like a stoney prairie; a rock riddled pothole region?

If you look closely at the clay, you will see in it streaks of black and others of yellow. How did they get there? I envision what I have always seen washing up on lake shores after a good wind; the black bits of bark and other plant debris forming windrows on beaches, the yellow and green waves of collected pollen clinging to shore. Is that what was in the clay? If so, there must have been forests growing near shore even then, leaving their telltale traces to be deciphered by those more learned than I. What they could learn from such records I could only guess but assume they would be able to at least determine the plant species from the pollen or plant residue.

A solid "thunk" and we would hit a boulder. Whoever was shoveling would try to pry it up while the other reached into the hole to retrieve it. If you are lucky it is not too large. If it is too big, the hole would have to be filled in and the process begun over. Most of the time, a brown stained rock would be pried to the top of the hole, sweaty arms and grimy hands assisting it. Unceremoniously the rock, bathed in sunlight for the first time in thousands of years, would be rolled into the underbrush. If it was a nice, flat one it would be saved specially to use as a footrest or step in front of the latrine. An ignominious use, even for a rock.

A good cross section of the canoe country's history could be seen by this point. First was the thin top soil, dark brown and laced with fine roots, then the subsoil, a light cocoa brown and more granular. Finally there would be the grey clay, extending down to the bottom of the hole, a hole which we rarely were able to dig deeper than three feet. At that depth we would punch the earth's crust, dinting blade on a surface that had been worn and weathered before even the dinosaurs lived.

On this hole would go the latrine, either by carefully prying up and moving the old wooden structure or assembling a new fiberglas model on a wooden base. In either case the old hole would be filled with the dirt from the new and, if a new latrine was used, the old wooden box would be dismantled and scattered far back in the woods. This was a necessity for if you left the pieces anywhere near the campsite, invariably someone would decide that this flat piece of lumber, urine soaked though it was, would make a fitting piece of camp furniture or, worse yet, a good surface on which to fillet fish. We've seen both.

The wilderness latrine, I believe, is a necessary evil. A person only has to stop in an overused Quetico campsite, where latrines are not provided, to see the need for such facilities. The campsites of the BWCAW, which receive ten times more visitors than its Quetico counterpart, would be unsightly and unsanitary without latrines.

During a thirty day exploration of the Quetico a few years back, Mary Jo and I stopped at one campsite on the north end of Kahshahpiwi Lake. Kahshahpiwi itself is part of an interesting geological phenomenon. Strung in a line from north to south are Cairn, Sark, Keefer and Kahshahpiwi lakes, narrow and steep banked on the east. Lying in a fault, a settled fracture in the earth's crust, these lakes are bounded by high cliffs.

This particular site was on a beautiful island. Crowned with the majestic red Norway pines it looked terribly inviting. While Mary Jo held the canoe, I went ashore to inspect the camp. I hastily retreated to the canoe. Behind every bush was a pile of human waste, strewn with toilet paper. Feminine hygiene products hung on bushes like grotesque Christmas ornaments. Obviously a large group had camped there for some time and just as obviously, not one person in that group had the brains necessary to dig a small hole for everyone to use.

I suppose it is not to be wondered at that most people don't know how to handle the wastes of their own bodily functions. In our every day existence we walk into a sanitary room and do our task, whisking it away with the flick of a lever. Most don't even know, or care, where that waste goes, and lordy, don't ask them about it. If there were no latrines in the BWCAW, that island camp we discovered on a well used Quetico route would seem like a garden spot in comparison to those on the U.S. side of the border.

There is a certain sense of satisfaction in creating anything, even a latrine. Mary Jo stated that with a latrine completed, she felt good because she could see the end results of her labors and that those labors produced something that worked. Whether or not she reaches her eighth graders she feels is a more nebulous question.

The final step in our latrine ritual was a ceremonial planting. Hiking far back into the forest I would find a small balsam fir and carefully remove it roots and all. After firmly tamping down the soil placed in the old latrine hole, the little tree would be carefully planted in its new, and remarkably fertile, home. A scattering of pine needles and other forest duff, as well as some of the sod cut from the location of the new latrine, would be laid in place around the migrated tree. With care, our landscaping job would leave the location of the old hole virtually indistinguishable from the surrounding forest.

We then spread a few handfuls of seed into the raw earth surrounding the new latrine. Hopefully in a few months the plants would grow up and mask the scars we had wrought on the fragile forest floor. The last task completed we both invariably turn one last time to admire our work, as if it were some impressive work of art.

If the latrine is a necessary evil, at least then we have learned something by digging them. We have seen in our carving of the earth the history written within. While we have unearthed no mastodon bones or ivory tusks, one can always hope. We have also learned just what a difficult task it is to dig a proper hole in the canoe country, amid its rocks and roots. We have acquired a deeper appreciation for this simple utility.

We have also discovered one other very important thing: don't dig the new hole just downwind of the old hole. The job is always more pleasant on the upwind side.

Paddled out to Fall Lake landing to resupply. Strong SW winds at over twenty miles per hour all day made the trip difficult and dangerous. Weather forced a 1½ hour layover near Caribou Point in Jackfish Bay, Basswood Lake.

Radioed Voyageur Visitor Center that we'd be late for our 3:30 p.m. pick-up. Finally arrived at 5:15.

•HOMEBOUND, WINDBOUND•

Mary Jo and Gypsy both snoozed in the rumbling old Landcruiser. I was fighting both sleep and traffic as we wheeled south from Ely toward Duluth, the old truck's maximum speed of fifty miles per hour a terrifying change of pace. It had been a very long day.

We had arrived late at our appointed meeting place with the Forest Service. The winds had been fearful and the seas high all day and we only made it out after sitting windbound on Caribou Point for an hour and a half.

This was our first trip back into civilization. Our food supplies had run low and we had been subsisting mostly on those dregs in the bottom of the food pack that are saved for last only because they are the least appetizing. While I can honestly say that I was not enamored with the idea of leaving the canoe country, even for just four days, the thought of fresh foods and a hot shower was very appealing.

It is probably the reason why we risked traveling on such a day as this. Even as we drove home and the winds had died down somewhat, the truck was constantly buffeted about. What we had experienced on the water had been much more frightening.

Naturally, the day you choose to travel large expanses of open water, the wind becomes your adversary. We had chosen to depart via the Basswood River and down Basswood Lake, taking the route through Jackfish Bay to Newton Lake and ending at Fall Lake. The Forest Service would meet us there and transport our equipment and us to our truck in town. If only it had been that simple.

If you were to look at a map of this route you would quickly see that the worst possible wind would be one from the southwest. Any other direction would allow you to hug a lee shore, even in a gale. Of course, today we had such a southwest wind.

The sensible thing to do would have been to wait things out, to camp on Basswood one more night and leave early in the morning. Why we continued to travel under such adverse conditions is beyond me, and really, beyond good judgment. Perhaps we were looking forward to pizza and beer more than we had thought, though they seem like ridiculous things to risk one's life on.

And that was virtually what we did. From the time we reached the narrows of north Jackfish Bay, we fought huge seas. At one point we paddled furiously only to hold position and the half mile from the narrows to the first sheltering island to the southeast took over a half an hour. We were no longer traveling in miles per hour, but feet per hour and any mistake or a broken paddle would have meant sure capsizing.

Even paddling within feet of shore did not help and when we had fought our way painstakingly down half of Pipestone Bay we were suddenly confronted with the worst of it. The seas, running near three feet, were too powerful to overcome and at times I remember having to look skyward to see Mary Jo as we climbed each wave as though it were a hill. Enough was enough. I knew we were licked.

The most terrifying moment though was trying to make land. We gradually slipped sideways to the west, a half mile south of Caribou Point, and prayed silently for a suitable landing site. At last there was no choice but to allow the canoe to go ashore, boulders or not, and take our chances. It would have to be done quickly to avoid smashing the canoe to pieces or losing our packs. We steeled ourselves, let the canoe ride a huge wave to the crashing beach and leapt overboard between the canoe and the boulders.

In water up to my waist I held the canoe with all my strength, the waves determined to wrest it away and send it to its doom. Mary Jo and Gypsy took a dunking and climbed to shallower water. The wind and waves were so loud we had to scream our conversation but no doubt the excitement also had something to do with our volume. Mary Jo turned and I tossed each pack haphazardly toward her. Though they were heavy, especially the one in which we were packing out over fifty pounds of non-burnable trash we had picked up, we managed to handle them as if they were light. With the canoe mostly empty I let the wind take the bow and when the stern swung toward shore, forced it through the bushes and to safety, Mary Jo tugging on it as she scrambled for footing on the steep slope. We were safe.

Climbing to the crest of the hill we sat exhausted on a rock shelf. Both of us were testy and exchanged some terse words, not so much because we were particularly angry with each other but because of the adrenalin pumping through our bodies. Mary Jo had been very frightened for our lives, as had been I, although most of my concern came from securing the safety of our belongings and the delay in our travel. Of the two of us, I'd say Mary Jo's fright was much more sensible.

After resting for a few minutes, letting the sun dry us somewhat, I retrieved the radio and called Voyageur Visitor Center in Ely. Gil Knight, a ranger on duty there and the one who would meet us at Fall Lake, advised us to stay put. The winds, he said, were at a constant twenty miles per hour with long, sustained gusts of over thirty. He would, he continued, meet us no matter what time we arrived and that we should wait until conditions were more favorable. He didn't need to tell me twice. I have little doubt we were the only fools trying to travel that day.

The day was really quite pleasant, despite the wind. Sitting and watching the combers march incessantly down the length of Pipestone Bay, I began to relax. Each wave was crested in white, a stark contrast to the indigo waters. Silver wisps of clouds tore across the sky, twisting and changing shape like foam in a rapids. The ledge we were on was crowned in jack pines and the wind shouted through their boughs. When I stand beneath a pine and hear the wind in its limbs I am always soothed. On the coldest of winter days, when all trees except the pines, firs and spruce are barren of foliage, and the wind stirs through their needles, I am invariably transported to some sunny, windy point in the canoe country.

I had forgotten an important lesson this day. I had struggled to make something happen, at great risk, that was unimportant, that could wait for another day. Determined to depart on this day, I had acted stupidly. What difference could it possibly make if we arrived in Ely one day late? We had enough food and would not starve. Even as I neared civilization I had succumbed to the pressures of it, its deadlines and schedules we all think are so inviolate. For three weeks I had a calendar for a watch, each day taking care of itself and the exact hour in which we arose, ate or slept not in the least important. Now I counted minutes and had an appointment to make and for no reason except that I had said we would be there at such and such a time, I had risked our safety.

Patience is an important lesson of nature. The sense of endless time one feels in the wilderness is not an illusion. Stripped of schedules, all things in the wild happen at a time appointed by conditions and opportunity. A wolf eats when it can, taking game when available. When the water lilies reach for the pond's surface a moose feeds on this delicacy, and not one moment before. A moose can neither choose the time of the lily's sprouting nor hurry it, and is content. When the wild rice is ripe, ducks and blackbirds can gorge themselves and though they may wish that season of plenty would come sooner and last longer, they waste no energy in worrying about it.

And so a canoeist should travel when it is calm and sit when it is windy, should build a fire when weather permits and eat a cold supper when all is wet. Frustration is a part of throwing yourself against a condition you can not change.

As the wind continued unabated, Mary Jo and I sat and munched gorp, reading paperbacks to pass the time. With the pressure of a deadline lifted, we began to enjoy the beautiful, though windy, day. There is a sense of ultimate leisure in this, which I had temporarily forgotten, much like the feeling one gets being in snug shelter during a blinding blizzard. Confined by the weather one needs no excuse to be lazy. No one will fault you for not traveling; indeed they will praise your intelligence for just sitting around. At any other time you would be labeled a bum, not a genius.

For an hour and a half Mary Jo and I were absolutely brilliant.

Saw Chip Elkins and partner off about 9:00 a.m. Unpacked food and gear.

Checked all campsites in immediate vicinity. Rained on and off all day.

♦ CALENDAR TIME ♦

It was a two pot of coffee morning. Mary Jo and I were tired from lugging in nearly a month's worth of groceries yesterday, all in a pouring rain, down the mile length of Horse Portage. It was a damn fine feeling to be back at the cabin, or, as we have nonchalantly found ourselves calling it, home. We had been very anxious to get back.

The trip to Duluth was pleasant enough and I doubt a shower ever felt better. But we ate too much junk food and opened too many envelopes that contained bills for either our bodies or minds to not feel worse for the trip.

The trip in was shortened by a tow up Jackfish Bay of Basswood Lake to the narrows north of which motors are banned. Fortunately ranger Pete Weckman was working in that area and consented to meet us at old Jimmy Pete's Landing at the south end of the bay. All of us rode in Pete's square stern canoe and towed our canoe loaded with packs. A wet ride over fair seas, it none the less saved us four or more hours of labor and was welcomed.

From the time we had been dropped off on our own until we reached the cabin the heavens let loose, not with thunderstorms and driving winds but a heavy, soaking rain that sought out every gap in our raingear. Even good raingear is almost useless in this kind of rain for with water running down your sleeves when you paddle or carry a canoe, as well as it seeking out the back of your neck, it is not long before both sources migrate and meet on your back. You're just going to get wet, so you might as well buck up, chum.

We had a welcoming committee waiting for us at the cabin and a very happy one at that. Ranger Chip Elkins radioed us just as we cleared Wheelbarrow Portage. Unable to reach us before that time, he was relieved to find we were so near. He and his partner had just come down the length of Crooked and had dreamed of a dry bed come night. Finding the cabin locked (there was a time you could leave a cabin in the wilderness unlocked, but no longer), they were becoming resigned to the fact that they must camp in the rain. Any other night it would have been just routine but to be so near to a dry shelter, only to find it locked, had heightened their exasperation.

Helping us with the heavy packs they accompanied us to the cabin where we all spread out our soaked gear. The two rooms were littered with wet shirts, pants and socks, hanging from every imaginable protrusion. When everyone had slipped into dry clothes we cooked a big dinner, a sense of contentment filling the cabin. Even though Chip is a full-time ranger, and technically our superior, he graciously deferred to us as if he were in our home, which, in a sense, he was. We talked well into the night, glad for the chance to air our problems with someone who could lend advice. I came to appreciate Chip's quiet humor and the imaginative ways he had devised to make this job easier. If all the rangers were of the caliber of Elkins and the few others we had met so far, I'd say the Forest Service was well staffed.

We saw them off from our dock in the rain this morning. It would be another wet day but we would have the cabin to dry out in and they would be in Ely by dark. Chip left a dozen leeches for me. This was a particularly precious commodity because the walleyes had been reluctant for some time now to feed on anything but live bait. Mary Jo and I had searched the area for worms and found few because of the thin soil and even trapping leeches (in an old coffee can with a fish head for bait) had proved futile. A dozen leeches wasn't many but I knew that if used sparingly on a reef I had found nearby, they would furnish us with a few meals of walleye.

We would eat well for a while. One of our packs is a specially constructed Forest Service model that housed a cooler in its depths.

In it we had packed bacon, eggs, venison steaks and chops and assorted cheeses and hard sausage. All of this food, except the eggs, had been frozen solid so no space would be wasted with ice. By opening and closing it quickly and only when we needed to retrieve something, some of this food would stay chilled for five days. During that time anything that would spoil once it warmed would be consumed, leaving those things that kept well without refrigeration for a later time.

The bulk of our food required no cooling and would keep indefinitely. Just about every meal had a base of noodles or rice and most of these were common grocery store foods. We had ranged all the aisles of the supermarket reading labels in preparation for this summer, looking for dried meals that required only water and margarine for cooking. When instructions called for milk, we simply added water and an appropriate amount of powdered milk.

Our only concession to high-tech camping foods came in the meat and vegetable department. Long after the fresh vegetables or meat had been consumed, we would be able to dine on dried products. Adding the freeze dried meat and vegetables to a packaged noodle dinner, we would create delicious one pot meals, much like a casserole. Before departing we had wrapped each meal separately so that only one bundle need be retrieved to create a meal. In that package might by some beef flavored noodles, a package of freeze dried beef and some dried peas. With a few dried onions and some spices, we had a passable stroganoff. Mary Jo had included many used 35mm film canisters filled with spices for they were light and took little space. Used creatively with the hodgepodge of other ingredients, we had been able to dish up some delectable dinners. In an oriental grocery in Duluth we had even found some dried shrimp, which added to a cold pasta salad and sprinkled with grated parmesan cheese, had been delicious.

There was always room for a few treats as well and as a chocolate fanatic, I had made sure a large Hershey bar was tucked neatly away. No-bake cheesecake was a special event as were instant puddings. The heaviest items were dried fruits and nuts. For some reason we have found that we have cravings for these things while we are in the bush, though we eat them only rarely at home.

I think our favorite meals to date have been those of fresh fish, primarily walleye or smallmouth bass. To prepare the fish we have packed in a supply of cooking oil and flour and cornmeal for batter. A few flaky white fillets, crisped to a golden perfection, and a loaf of fresh baked bread or bannock can content the most voracious voyageur.

Breakfast consisted largely of oatmeal once the bacon and eggs had been consumed. Occasionally we started the morning with pancakes as well but found the oatmeal to stick with us longer and be quicker to prepare. Crackers, bread, cheese, hard salamis, granola bars and gorp were our luncheon entrees.

In case of medical emergency, such as snake bite, we also packed in a couple of quarts of medicinal alcohol, namely brandy and scotch.

We had managed to get all of this food, and more, into two and a half packs, each one weighing about fifty pounds. The half pack of food contained the cooler and on top of it went two gallons of fuel for our stoves and lanterns. Subtracting the weight of those, and of the cooler itself, our food probably weighed in at just over one hundred pounds. Since we will be staying in for twenty-four days before resupplying, that averages out to a little over two pounds of food per person per day. Gypsy carried her own dog food which, at a pound per day, meant her pack was over twenty pounds. Considerable planning, measuring and repackaging is necessary to trim your needs down to two pounds a day. I doubt if we could have done this as efficiently as we have had we not taken a thirty day canoe trip the year before. Unknown to us at the time, it was a perfect training trip for this summer.

Meals are an event in the bush. Hungry after a hard day's work or travel, all voyageurs stare impatiently at the blackened pot simmering over the fire. There are foods that take less time to cook than others, but few, if any, are truly instant. Time is required to gather wood, build a fire and bring the ingredients to a boil and there are no shortcuts, save using a stove. While we always carry a small stove with us, we prefer to cook over a wood fire and luxuriate in the leisure it affords. The food is good but it is the leisure that is so delicious. Wood

is plentiful so there is no need to hurry to conserve fuel and a campfire allows us to bake a loaf of bannock, a hard thing to due properly on a stove.

Back at the cabin, we were ready to again experience that unhurried pace. For over three weeks we would have no pressing appointments, no schedule to follow. Certainly there were jobs to complete and places to go but they would happen in a loosely structured way. With a general plan in mind we would complete those tasks, but do them at the time and pace wind and weather would allow.

I knew that if we stayed out here long enough we would slip back into the ancient rhythm that had governed man's movements for hundreds of thousands of years. Sleep would come when we were tired, meals when we were hungry. A glance at the sky would be enough to tell time; knowing whether it was morning or afternoon precise enough. Had this place been our permanent abode, no doubt we would have been encompassed by these rhythms even further, with weekends being no different than weekdays and seasons more important than months.

I pitied Chip and his partner, slogging their way up the Horse River. It was pouring again, a steady curtain of water streaming over the eaves of the cabin, past our window. Mary Jo brought us another cup of coffee.

I took off my watch. We would not have the chance to let months run in to seasons, but we could let the days become blurs. We were ready to go back to telling time with a calendar.

Brushed area to the west and north of the cabin as well as trail to boathouse. The work we did near the cabin opens it up to the lake and sky, letting in both more light and cheer. "Mowed" the lawn around the cabin with the grass whip.

Inspected all the campsites in the area to see how they fared while we were gone. Broke up abandoned illegal camp on Lower Falls portage. Made many contacts with campers.

◆ MAKING TIME ◆

Hurriedly the group of four loaded their two canoes at the bottom of the Canadian portage around the falls. Apparently seeing the Forest Service logo on our canoe or lifejackets as we sat in our canoe watching, they paddled quickly over to us and pulled alongside our canoe, grasping the gunwale.

"Can you tell us how long it will take to reach Friday Bay?" asked the man who apparently was their group leader.

I scanned their equipment. Sleek and low, their canoes were built for speed as long as they did not have to fight big seas. The day was calm. In their hands each held a feather light, bent shaft, graphite paddle. The packs all were new and of the latest high-tech design. Each member of the party had the healthy look of athletes. They looked as though they could travel fast.

Before I could reply, the group leader breathlessly began to speak again.

"We got windbound yesterday on Basswood, trying to cross Bayley Bay. Threw our whole schedule off. We'd like to reach Lac La Croix by tomorrow and head out through Nina Moose the next day. Damn wind. Had to sit around all day."

"Say, isn't there something to see around here, some Indian paintings or something like that?"

I was pooped out just listening to him. He reminded me of some pent up, nervous animal, just ready to break.

I was just about to respond when he started up once more.

"By the way, could you recommend a good campsite down there, one not too far out of the way? Don't want to spend too much time lookin' around. Like to make camp fast so we can get a good night's sleep. Gotta get going early tomorrow," he said, twirling his paddle in his hands. He must have noticed my watching this.

"Yep, these paddles sure are nice. Weigh just a couple of ounces each. We can travel faster than ever now. Just picked them up before this trip. Bought the canoe last year. With this canoe and these paddles we can really make time. Been lookin' forward to this trip."

I took a deep breath.

"I'd say you'll make Friday Bay in about four hours if you don't stop along the way. Hand me your map, I'll point out the pictographs and a campsite."

I showed him what he wanted on the map and barely retrieved my finger before he folded the parchment and shoved it in a pack pocket. In a flurry of paddles they were away, racing down the river to the lake. Mary Jo and I sat a while and watched, floating in the foam below the falls, listening to its song.

We are back into the swing of things.

Went to Wednesday Bay and back today. Cleaned sites and watched the young eagle in nest 321E. Almost as if we had never left, it was standing in exactly the same place on the nest's edge as it had been the last time we passed through.

We also spotted one of the few other wood and canvas canoes we've seen this summer, a beautiful boat built by Joe Seliga of Ely.

• THE WIDJI WAY •

There was no mistaking it. Pulled up on the gently sloping shelf of granite that spreads wide at the base of Table Rock was the graceful form of a wood canoe. As we cruised by a ray of sun shot from between two clouds and struck the campsite, bathing the canoe in light. The craft's cedar interior glowed butterscotch.

Since we are devotees of the wooden canoe, and they are fairly rare these days, we paddled to shore to take a closer look. As we neared, a young man in his early twenties walked to the water's edge, followed by four teenage boys. Seeing the wooden canoe, the guide and the boys, I knew immediately then that they were from Camp Widjiwagan outside Ely, one of the many camps that send thousands of youths into the canoe country each year.

We introduced ourselves to the young guide and he helped us ashore. Unlike most who try to assist us, much to my consternation, by dragging the canoe fully loaded across the rocks, this young fellow waited until we stepped out into the water and then helped me lift the canoe clear and set it gently down. He knew how to treat a canoe, especially a wood canvas canoe.

I had been impressed with most of the groups we had seen this summer from Widjiwagan. They almost always traveled in two canoes in groups of no more than five people, like this one. Unlike some other camps that each dispatch hordes of kids each summer, mostly in groups of ten and often with what we considered very poor supervision, the groups from Widjiwagan were usually small and had always appeared well guided. The other groups were sometimes announced from miles away by the banging of aluminum canoes on rocks and the screaming of teenagers, disturbing every other camper and the wildlife. Parties from Widjiwagan came and went quietly, almost as if they had never been there, leaving no sign of there passing.

While this is something that should not have to be wondered at, it too often is. Not leaving any sign of your passing, making no impression on other campers or the land should be the rule in wilderness travel. More than anything this is a lesson the youth camps should be teaching, trying to instill a respectful land ethic. Wilderness is the perfect place for this lesson for if children can not learn to respect the land here, what hope is there?

I have heard the guides from Widjiwagan express this ethic as the "Widji Way." It is as good a name as any and in their case it is not simply dogma, but a fact. I have watched them come and go all summer.

A great part of this, I believe, begins with their use of wooden canoes. Widjiwagan has a great store of wood canvas canoes dating back many decades, each one the veteran of untold wilderness canoe trips. Those who think wood canvas canoes are delicate things need only inquire as to the history of some of these wonderful old boats to know that they are as durable as they are beautiful. But they do need, like the land, to be treated respectfully.

We choose to paddle such a canoe. Built for us by Alex Comb of Stewart River Boatworks in Two Harbors, Minnesota, this replica of the famed Chestnut Cruiser has a lineage better than my own. One of the designs that had opened up the north country across all the Great Lake states and Canada, it is as much a part of the canoe country as those trees from which it came. The successor to the birch bark canoe of the Indians, it is for the most part, made of the cedar that rims the lakes of the northland. When we paddle that canoe we feel a link to nature.

I have watched groups from Widjiwagan approach a portage. The canoe is unloaded while it floats, never touching land, the youths standing up to their knees in water, passing the packs to shore. When unloaded, the canoe is lifted from the lake, carried through the forest and set down gently, in the water. There is no noise, no grating of aluminum or fiberglas on rock, no telltale bits of ground up canoe on boulders to mark their passing. Even when one of their canoes is not wood, it is treated with equal care. If all visitors to the wilderness took such care, it would be better for it.

Because a wooden canoe is so beautiful, and because its canvas skin does require some consideration, the respect shown for it has a tendency to carry over to a respect for the land. This land ethic is very important for it is an attitude that must be developed in all of us before we succeed in fouling the entire planet. When we build things that are indestructible, and there is a difference between indestructible and merely durable, we sometimes put ourselves at odds with nature. If your canoe is tougher than the canoe country granite, will you still defer to it? Will you concede to it the eons it has known, the history that it has seen or will you deal it a blow?

But a land ethic is more than this. Developing a respect for the land means realizing that you are a part of it and not separate from it. That all things, living or not, are so intertwined as to be as the weave of a fabric. When we begin to unravel this cloth, as now seems to be the rule in this troubled world, it weakens so that eventually it is no more than gauze. When we have pulled one thread too many from this fabric, it will disintegrate around us and no one will be able to piece it back together again.

It is as if by the very virtue of being human, we believe that we can do what we may, simply because it is possible or convenient and not because it is needed or right. I see this egocentricity on a small scale here, in small, unthinking acts. If we teach it is right to bathe ourselves in a pristine lake, or do our dishes there, or to use it to dispose of waste or fish offal, what consequences will these lessons have once we leave the wilderness? It may be a only a bar of soap here but the message is the same: we have the right to pollute. The difference between washing your dishes in a lake and flushing your city's waste water into the Mississippi River is only a matter of degree.

I know the feeling that each of us has, that we are unable to stem this dirty tide, that our actions alone are meaningless. This is a dangerous trap for if individuals cease to try, how can the race as a whole succeed? Let us each build our own land ethic first, stone by stone as if in a wall, and we may find that this fence is substantially complete, our neighbors busy building too all the while we struggled.

It starts with respect. It begins with learning that each animate being and inanimate thing has a right to exist and that you can not change the least of these without affecting the whole. This right to exist also includes the need to use, as in a deer browsing a sapling or a man or wolf killing and eating that deer. Such acts must be kept in balance, and to do so, mankind needs to understand his dependency on nature. Without nature, man would perish both spiritually and physically. Nature is far more important to us than we are to it, and would flourish in our absence. We are but as a baby at its mother's breast, and are totally dependent.

A lot to infer, maybe, from the way a group treats its canoes. Perhaps, but this camp was clean and quiet, filled with impressionable teens who were absorbing an important lesson in respect. I felt optimistic as we left, for they had been taught the Widji way. Maybe we should send the whole world to Camp Widjiwagan.

Went east up the Basswood River and worked on Horse Portage today clearing deadfalls, repairing rock work and removing brush.

Spent some time inspecting latrines; a lovely job on a hot day. Quite a few will need replacing.

The weather has grown hot and with the heat the blueberries are ripening quickly now. Gypsy flushed a family of grouse on the portage.

Took the time to talk with the many campers passing through.

• TACT •

During our rounds today we encountered many groups, and took the opportunity to talk to each. We try never to let a party pass by without making an attempt to chat with them.

Dealing with the public takes a great deal of tact sometimes. By far, most people we have encountered have been pleasant, peaceful voyageurs and I often have to remind myself of that fact. Those who have been less than thoughtful of the wilderness, or downright disrespectful, have made a greater impression on us and have unjustly twisted our opinion. Some of our most pleasant moments have come sharing a campfire and a cup of coffee with travelers, answering a myriad of questions and lending assistance where we could.

Even the majority of those who we have discovered doing something illegal or harmful have been doing it primarily from ignorance. This gives us the perfect opportunity to discuss proper behavior in the wilderness and most take it in the spirit in which it was given and we part as friends. Some have even stopped by later to thank us and we feel amply rewarded. One couple even went so far as to claim we were the highlight of their trip. If that were so, they must not have had a very good time.

Not that I haven't put my foot in it on a couple of instances. A few samples will suffice.

"I notice that you have a dog with you," one woman stated as we floated on the river offshore her camp. "Is that common for rangers?"

"Oh yes ma'am," I answered matter-of-factly. "Gypsy here is a standard issue, USFS labrador retriever. We use them mostly for bear control and search and rescue. Each two person team has one dog."

"Well, my goodness, isn't that something!" she declared excitedly. "Wait 'till I tell our friends back home."

Oh, oh. I realized I had gone too far, never believing for a moment that she might not guess I was pulling her leg. I sheepishly told her I was only kidding. She didn't laugh.

Two fellows flagged us down one day as we were returning to the cabin, seeking advice. We stopped in front of their camp in shallow water, a convenient rock shelf four inches below the surface, and stepped out in our rubber bottom, leather topped water tight boots. As I was standing in the water, one hand on the canoe to keep it from floating away, I happened to look down during the conversation. There was something on the lake bottom.

"Oh for pete's sake," I exclaimed, "look what some asshole did. They threw broken eggs in the lake!"

"Um, ah, I did that," said one of the pair standing on shore. "They broke in our pack."

"What the hell does this lake look like to you, a goddamn garbage can?" I retorted angrily.

Ooops. Too far again. It is pretty hard to get fired from a volunteer position but I might just succeed if I kept this up. I apologized.

"Is there much wildlife around here?" a woman inquired one evening as we talked in the campsite below the cabin.

"You bet," I said. "There are eagles nesting just across from this camp, above the falls. We've seen quite a few moose and deer as well. Of course, there are black bears around."

"Bears! Where? Here? You mean there are bears near this camp?"

"Yes ma'am. We've seen two different ones. A smaller one around two hundred pounds and a big one I'd guess would go closer to three-fifty."

The woman was clearly growing excited.

"And you just let them wander around? Why don't you trap them and move them someplace else?"

This one hit me right between the eyes. My jaw flopped open in disbelief.

"Jesus, lady. Where the hell would you like us to put them? We're in the wilderness already," I answered heatedly.

Definitely not very tactful. Maybe I should have apologized, but I didn't. I even gave some thought to coming back in the middle of the night and growling outside of their tent. Of course, I wouldn't do that.

I could see the headlines of the Ely Echo now: Chicago Woman Clubs Volunteer Ranger Over the Head in BWCAW. "He was growling outside my tent during the night," she told reporters. "I thought he was a bear. Thank goodness I brought a piece of firewood into the tent."

Yes sir. A little more tact on my part could save me a lot of trouble.

Stopped, checked and cleaned a few campsites, made some camper contacts but basically, took most of the day off.

Explored the reedy, shallow bays northwest of the cabin. Spotted one bald eagle and many ducks, most of which appear to have had very good hatches this year. Found some good walleye fishing on a reef nearby, the location of which shall remain a secret.

Had a strange event occur after dark. At 10 p.m. this evening we had four boys from the site behind the cabin come over, terrified. While their group leader was out for a late paddle, one of the teenage boys in the camp pulled a knife on the others. Said "it was time" and that he was going to kill them.

I went to the campsite, took the knife from the boy, sent him into his tent and told him to get into his sleeping bag. I threatened to sit on his chest until the counselor returned if he did not keep quiet. Sat with the other boys until the leader returned.

◆ RINGNECK BAY ◆

If I had been an Indian, and this were autumn, I would have chosen this little island for a campsite. It did not afford a majestic vista, nor was it particularly striking in and of itself, but it offered something I'm sure someone living off the land would consider far more important: food.

A quarter mile from the main channel and a half mile north of the falls, the island sat between two reed choked paths through the bay. To the west of the little island grew one of the very few stands of wild rice we had seen in this area. Although it was a small patch of rice, I doubt it would have been overlooked by anyone who valued this nutritious grain as much as had the Ojibway. A few hours work come early September and the rice would have been harvested. Even if it had filled only a few birch bark containers, it just might have been the difference between health or hunger if the coming winter were severe.

The rice alone would not have been the sole reason for a family of hunter-gatherers to camp here. Because of the rice, ducks surely would have stopped here in numbers and even today, two months before the waterfowl would begin their annual migration, we were treated to the sight and sound of dozens of ducks. The direct correlation between wild rice and ducks had not been lost on the Indians and they both shot them with their arrows and used nets to trap them. Anyone who has ever feasted on the sweet meat of a wild rice fattened black duck would understand both the need and the pleasure of the Ojibway in gathering a few ducks.

Most of the ducks we have seen have been ringnecks, but there have also been mallards, black ducks and the fish eating mergansers. All of them have had respectable hatches and we watched in amazement as one valiant ringneck hen attacked our canoe as we crept through the reeds. So suddenly did she come upon us, and so intense was her charge, that we barely noticed the scurrying ducklings heading for deeper cover. Of course this was exactly why she rowed so furiously across the water's surface, bearing her breast to our bow and quacking excitedly. In those few seconds she had so brazenly risked her own life, her young had found safety.

A mallard hen nested this summer on the portage island at Lower Basswood Falls. One afternoon as I searched the island for a member of a party that had camped illegally there, I nearly stumbled upon her nest. Unseen by me, the hen had sat staunchly until I was about to set foot on her and then launched herself through the maze of branches toward the river. I nearly stumbled over backwards in my fright at the sudden commotion and when I realized what had happened, looked around for her nest. Exactly where I would have placed my next step was a beautifully crafted nest the size of a dinner plate. In it were the mallard's eggs, white as a store bought chicken egg and about the same size. I was thankful I had not stepped on them and ruined an entire year's effort.

The hen was fortunate as well that I was not a fox or other predator as those eggs would certainly have not lasted long once she had left. No doubt her choice in nesting on this rapids surrounded island was no accident. Choosing an island would help to insure that such egg robbers would be less likely to find her nest. It seemed reasonable that few of them would risk swimming the fast water on the off chance the little island might hold such a meal.

Of the eight eggs she had in that nest, I know of six that had hatched successfully. One day I watched her parade her yellow and brown ducklings through the fast water beneath the falls, the little ducks floating so high and lightly that they seemed to almost bounce off the chop. Still later I saw the family and they were down to five chicks, and yet later, four. I do not know what happened to the missing little ones but I might guess that the big pike that swim beneath the falls had accounted for at least one.

Besides rice and ducks, the little island campsite in the bay would offer a chance at even more important food. Because of the rich aquatic environment, moose often frequent this bay. So much of the river nearby is surrounded by steep, rocky banks or enveloped in fast moving water, that few water lilies grow. But in this secluded bay lilies grew in profusion. Both large and small yellow water lilies were present and the even more spectacular white lily with its saucer-like leaves crowded the waterways. Moose find these plants a delicacy and continue to feed on their root systems until October when these big deer suddenly move to feeding on browse in the highlands. As delectable as the moose found the lilies, I'm sure the Ojibway found the moose. And in the sudden violent death of a moose, an Indian father could feed his family for many, many days.

We have not seen many moose this summer, owing to the fact that we spend so much time either on big water or fast river where they do not frequent. Yet we have seen much sign of their passing, including three different carcasses of moose that had fallen through last winter's ice, and every portage trail yields a clue of their coming and going to the observant.

In a quiet bay to the east of the confluence of the Horse and Basswood Rivers we watched a large, dark cow moose feed serenely.

We were just leaving a campsite in that bay, nearly a third of a mile distant, when we spotted her, very nearly black against the pale green willows and sedges. I do not think we would have known it was a moose except for the movement and when we saw her lift her head from feeding below the surface, we saw the sparkling waters drip from her massive muzzle and mule-like ears. We paddled over quietly, moving as an Indian might, timing our strokes with her dunkings until we were just twenty yards away.

Only then did we see the two buff colored calves standing in the reeds behind her. They must have been watching our approach the whole time because when we spotted them they were already staring wide-eyed at us. This time, when the cow came up for air, she must have sensed her calves' alarm and swung to glare at us. We stayed absolutely motionless and watched as she flared her nostrils wide in an attempt to catch our scent, stringy lily roots dripping from her jaws, frozen in mid-chew. With a quartering wind between us and the moose I was sure she could not smell us but she knew something was amiss and leisurely herded her young into the willows behind. I have never been able to figure out how an animal as large as a moose can move through such dense cover as quietly as they do, but when these three had gone scarcely twenty yards into the brush the sound of their passing faded completely, leaving only the whipping willow tops to betray their passage.

A week later we saw what I would guess to be the same cow and calves. Talking to some campers in a site just northeast of the mouth of the Horse River, I was just answering a woman's question about moose. She wondered aloud where they might see one and I was just about to tell her of some good locations they could try when the cow and calves jumped into the river just above Lower Basswood Falls.

We all watched breathlessly as the three swam from Canada to the U.S., very near to the brink of the falls. Although moose are powerful swimmers with coats of hollow hair that allow them to float quite high, I was worried about the two little ones cutting across that powerful current. If the mother had guessed wrong and had led them into the river too near to the cataract, the calves may be swept to their death. Fortunately for the moose, and to the relief of all watching, the mother possessed good judgment.

All animals come to the water's edge more frequently when the insects are bad, seeking refuge either in the water or under it. While Mary Jo, Gypsy and I once paddled down the meandering Jean Creek north of Quetico's giant Sturgeon Lake, we surprised the largest bull moose I have ever seen. Completely submerged, for the deer and horse flies were atrocious that day, the old bull lay crocodile-like with only his rack and muzzle above the water. We may have paddled completely past without ever seeing him had he not chosen just that moment to get up. And up and up.

Black, with water streaming from his shiny coat, the huge palmated antlers in dark velvet swung toward us menacingly. When we were just about to start back paddling furiously, he turned and crashed into the jack pines, head high and antlers back.

Although the canoe country does not have a large whitetail deer population, we have seen more than I would have thought. Deer are primarily animals of younger forests and the BWCAW's timber is growing mature since it was logged fifty years ago. Much of the Quetico was never logged. But we have seen more deer than moose and most of them have been feeding along the water almost as if they had taken lessons from their much bigger cousin. I have never heard of deer feeding in the water but twice in one day in a sheltered area of the north part of Wednesday Bay we watched as the deer in their red coats fed in marshy coves. One was a large buck and with his huge rack still in velvet he was the epitome of beauty and grace. A nimble doe fed with him. Still later we watched another doe feed just a mile to the south.

The other day, while heading toward Horse Portage, we were very much surprised to see twin fawns along the Canadian shore opposite the Horse River. As we watched they gingerly crept through the brush, down to the river, and drank. Although getting quite large, the white spots of spring could still be seen faintly on their tawny coats. Mary Jo handled the canoe deftly from the bow, Gypsy intently staring at the deer, while I quickly retrieved my camera from a pack. Even though

the wind blew from our canoe to them, they seemed unalarmed. It would have been strange enough had only Mary Jo and I been in the canoe, but with the dog's scent blowing to them, I was very surprised they did not flee. Perhaps I am wrong, but I would guess a dog must smell very much like a wolf.

They allowed us to watch them feed and drink and at no time was there any sign of the doe that bore them. They seemed large enough now to take care of themselves even if something unfortunate had happened to their mother, but unless they grew a bit more wary they would not last too long. We appreciated their trust though, and watched until they faded back into the pines, the larger nubbin buck leading the way, occasionally turning to watch us over his shoulder.

Before leaving the little bay of my imagined Indian campsite, we turned north to an arm that ends abruptly beneath a large beaver dam. As we neared we flushed an eagle from a rock in the reeds, its white pate flashing in the sun, a fish dangling in its talons. Though startled, the eagle retained enough composure to remember to take its lunch.

As if ducks and eagles were not enough birds to see, we watch in disbelief as a giant amongst blue herons rose from beneath the beaver dam. I had seen the grey stark form of what I had supposed was an upright log beneath the dam and never for a moment supposed it could be a heron. When this bird took flight, its ungainly legs dangling behind and long neck tucked "S" shaped against its breast, it was obviously huge, bigger than I could have ever thought a heron could be.

"Look at that, Hon," I whispered to Mary Jo. "That's no heron, that's a damn pterodactyl!"

And so it looked to me, croaking as it flew.

As rich as the entire canoe country is in wildlife, this bay was even richer, a special place of slow waters, deeper soils and nutritious plants that was a oasis of life to all the creatures that call this hard land home. Although the thousands of tourists that paddle down the river on their way to Crooked Lake pass by with hardly a glance, I felt I was correct in my guess that it was a fertile feeding ground for not only the animals, but the Indians as well. They would have sought it out for a few days in autumn, I am sure.

I made a vow that someday I would come back when the leaves were changing, come back to see just how good the wild rice crop was and listen to the wings of ducks. Summer is a time of leisure here. It would take the feeling of the impending rush of winter to know the importance of such a bay.

My birthday. Worked some, played some.

Sealed the seams on the leaky tent issued to us, hoping that it corrects the problem. Did some trail brushing and worked on boathouse door.

Having nearly run out of leeches for bait, and having poor luck trapping more, I resorted today for searching for worms. After an hour I finally found one lonely nightcrawler. Didn't have the heart to take it.

◆ GIFTS ◆

With almost the hush of a gentle snowfall, the evening drifted down around us, enveloping everything and everyone in a blanket of darkness. So quiet was the calm that the remaining sounds became intense, the rustle of my clothing, the song of the falls, the pulsing of night insects filling my consciousness. They were so pervasive it was as if the sounds were trapped within and my ears were stuffed with cotton.

Gypsy lay snoozing in the bottom of the canoe, curled in a half moon, her head up between the pads of the yoke. She has a peculiar way of locking her head in that yoke, her muzzle across one pad and the back of her skull wedged against the other, that allows her to go limp and still stay in place. It does not look comfortable to me but she must find it so for she sleeps soundly in that position.

Mary Jo sat in the bow, hunched, her head drooping. I suspected she was dozing as well for her grip on her fishing rod was very loose. You learn to sleep in odd positions in the canoe country.

The stillness of the evening was narcotic, lulling everything into a peaceful slumber. I was still awake in the stern, half of my attention turned to my fishing, the other to my musing. The canoe drifted lazily, quietly. Even without an anchor we hadn't moved three feet in the

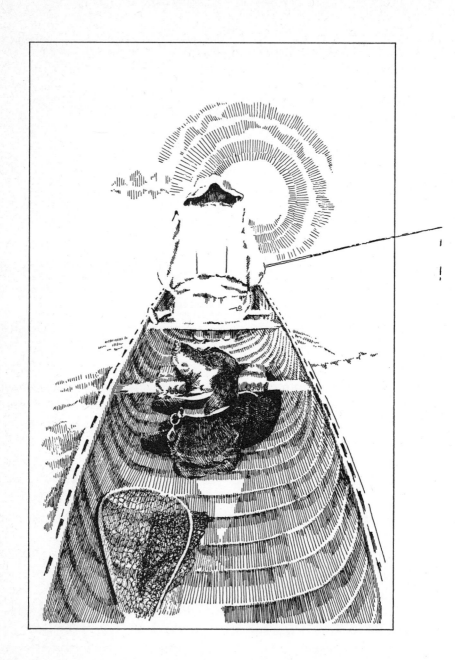

last half hour, positioned over our favorite nearby walleye reef. Unfortunately the walleyes seemed to be sleeping as well.

I did not find that to be a problem. Today was my birthday and I was just glad to be here, spending my birthday in a way that suits me. Fish or no, I was enjoying myself.

This was the first birthday I had spent in the woods for a long time and it reminded me of those of my childhood. Although I sometimes felt cheated of parties and friends at the time, I realize now just how special those birthdays were. I recall birthdays on Little Saganaga Lake, the Seagull River, Isle Royale and in the wild Nipigon country. Each one was marked only by a single candle on a cupcake my mother had smuggled along, maybe a song and probably a day of fishing. Birthday gifts would have to wait until we returned home, something that seemed like an eternity to me.

I realize now though that the real gift I received from my parents was a love for the wild. Can you imagine a more beautiful place to spend your birthday than the Seagull River? Although I did not have friends to invite to a party, I was not alone. One birthday was spent feeding blueberries to a family of black ducks. For such a wary bird these were amazingly tame and would almost eat from my hand. Some parties have children bobbing for apples, mine had ducks bobbing for blueberries, and I enjoyed immensely watching them scurry for the berries I tossed into the river. The party went on for hours.

Looking back I realize I never felt denied that our family seldom stayed in hotels or went to theme parks. No theme park can compare to the wild and my father, desperate for some peace during his too short vacation, would take our family to the woods; kids, dogs and all. We looked like a troop of gypsies and felt as free.

On weekends we would vacate to the woods as well. In the spring it was brook trout fishing, during the summer, canoe trips, campgrounds and fishing. Come fall my father would take me hunting and the lessons he taught about respecting all life ring true yet. It was under his guidance that I learned just how fleeting life was, how we fit into nature's scheme and that even though we killed, we must do so with reverence and take only what we could use.

Long after the birthday gifts of my childhood friends are worn and tossed aside, I cherish mine and use them daily. I do not remember what things I received on my fourteenth birthday but I do recall that my father and I portaged into Tuscarora Lake and can envision the giant pike I saw lazing along a reef in the crystalline waters. You can be considered wealthy if you gather memories instead of merely things.

Today I was thankful for those gifts of love and knowledge given to me by my parents. There is little doubt I would be a much different person without them. I was also thankful for the woman who sat in the bow of our canoe, without whose indulgence this three month gift of wilderness would not have been possible. A lucky voyageur has a good bow paddler and a fortunate husband has a patient wife. Doubly lucky then am I to have both in one special partner.

Clouds were scudding in from the west, their bellies lit by the few rays of the sun that peeked over the hillside. Pink and grey, the puffy sheet looked as if someone had strolled along the top, mounds punched into the underside. As the sun set completely a light breeze stirred from the north, just strong and cool enough to ruffle the blanket-like calm of the evening. Gypsy stirred in the bottom of the canoe, brown eyes opening as her nose worked the new air. She appeared to have a crick in her neck.

"Mary Jo," I said softly, unwilling to break the spell, "time to reel up and head in."

"Are you sure you want to? We can stay awhile. It's your birthday."

I looked at her. She was still half asleep, slumped so low that her life jacket rode up almost to her ears. I smiled in the darkness.

"That's OK, Hon. Enough's enough. Let's head in. It's been a great day."

We paddled slowly into the dark. The bats were out, swooping fast and low over the water, eating mosquitoes. I silently cheered them on. In the east the stars were shining beyond the approaching clouds. Lower Basswood Falls rumbled.

Somewhere on the river the loons began to sing, slowly then wildly, echoing everywhere. Nice touch, I thought. What's a birthday without a little singing?

Another day, another latrine.

We put in a new latrine at Basswood River site #1 (Horse Portage). Tough digging. Must have tried twenty times with the soil auger before finding enough soil. The soil here is hard and thin, evidence of the area's relatively recent glacial history.

Many folks traveling the famous Horse Portage today and we spent much time talking with them, lending both advice and directions as asked for. They seem glad to see us (Rangers, that is) and make use of us. It gives us much satisfaction to be able to be of help.

The weather was warm, the sky fair. Parts of the portage are now literally lined with luscious, ripe blueberries.

•PORTAGES•

One could say that a portage is simply an obstacle, something to toil over, the proverbial pain in the neck. Large loads carried sweatily over a rocky or wet portage is a task that some simply endure and having done so, swear that they will never do so again.

Portages can be that, or they can be something far different. We have come to look at portages with a different perspective, and each portage now is approached with a mixture of philosophy and realism. In any event, they are something that we no longer worry about and often look forward to.

A portage, long or short, taken after a tiring paddle into the teeth of the wind has become a welcome respite, the chance to use other muscles than those of the arms and shoulders and to stretch the legs. Sometimes being on the water can be frightening, as when the seas are running at the limit of your abilities or threatening weather looms ominously. At such times being on solid ground under the safety of canopied trees is comforting, for man is a creature of the firmament and even those who are nearly as comfortable on water as on land find solace on a surface that can not wet or sink his precious lifeline of equipment nor engulf him in an element that can rob life.

Portages are actually essential to a canoe trip. The canoe was invented not so much because it is the best of watercraft but because it is the best of watercraft that can be carried from lake to lake or river to river. The landscape contributed as much to the configuration of the canoe as did the water. If there had been no need for a portable boat, would there ever have been a canoe?

Portages then are part of a canoe trip and, on some routes, might actually be half of your trip. If you have been on the Quetico's Delahey death march, you know the truth of that. All voyageurs know of places where you swear that you spent as much time under a canoe on land as you did in the canoe on water. Don't look then upon portages as an inconvenience; look at them as part of the excitement and challenge and they will never again be dreaded.

Of course all of this depends on how smartly you have packed and your propensity to enjoy strenuous exercise.

You will never catch me jogging or in a health club pumping iron. I do not enjoy sit-ups. You will catch me, however, sweating along under a load on a portage, smiling mostly and often whistling. There is a simple joy in moving all your gear, those sparse items that give you freedom to be at home wherever your campfire glows, across a portage. It is exercise with a purpose and exercise with leisure.

Mary Jo and I don't have the luxury of packing lightly this summer. Besides all the normal camping gear every voyageur packs, we are always loaded down with saws, axes, shovels, pry bars, brooms and a host of other tools that are made principally of iron. Lots of iron. If ever there was a time that we should dread portages, it is this summer. Have you ever portaged a latrine, even if it has been dismantled?

That was our task this day, lugging lumber, the fiberglas shell and all of our tools up nearly the length of Horse Portage.

Instead we have learned that to each task there must be a certain amount of time allotted. It can not be completed in any less time than it takes. A simple revelation but one people fight every day. We each take on more than we can handle and struggle to fit it into a day, doing no job well and all uncomfortably. Being in the canoe country this summer has taught us something about patience, about leisure and about taking a task to completion naturally.

And portages are one of those tasks. The Horse Portage, a famous portage of nearly a mile in length that has been used for centuries bypassing the dangerous rapids of the upper Basswood River, is one that most people dread. It is a measure of a camper's endurance and attitude and I have found it interesting to watch those we have seen crossing this ancient trail.

One strapping young man reached the west end of the portage shortly after we had landed. He stumbled down the last little incline to the water and fairly throwing his pack into the bushes he dropped to his knees at the river's edge, plunging his head into the water. Sputtering, he cupped mouthful after mouthful of muddy water, still stirred up from our landing and unloading, to his face, drinking and gasping. His t-shirt was soaked with sweat and his athletic shorts were grimy, as if he had fallen on the portage. High top basketball sneakers were unlaced half-way, their tongues lolling out.

I don't think he even saw us until he sat back on his haunches and in a dazed expression he turned to us. He was a mess.

"Where's the nearest McDonalds? I need a Coke."

How do you answer a question like that? I suppose you could consider it a funny remark but there was no frivolity in this young man's voice. He was dead serious. The world he knew, the world of instant food, cold drinks and comfort was gone. He might have been on a distant planet for all he knew. He had a thirst the water of the Basswood could not slake for his thirst was for a different place. He was tired and in an alien environment and for all I knew, facing extended physical labor for the first time in his life. To him this portage had been a fearsome thing.

That this could be an alien environment to someone is a concept hard for me to grasp. I have spent a lifetime in the canoe country and other wild places and have come to feel more at home in the bush than anywhere else. I am a product of my father's love of the woods and the fact that the city I grew up in, Duluth, is heavily wooded. There never was a lack of things for my friends and me to do, not as long as there was a bag lunch in our packs and some forgotten patch of woods to explore. None of us were unaffected by those experiences.

Here though, was a child of the city. A young man who had never been in the woods, knew the annoyance of insects or the glory of a morning frost glazing the alder bottoms. America as a whole has grown more urbanized and while this boy's parents may have moved to the big city from a small town or farm, his generation had never wandered the forest, never crouched beside a stream watching for feeding trout. Not knowing the wild he dreads it. Not knowing the wild, he can not value it. This is a serious matter for as our countrymen turn away from the wilderness, do not remember land, air or water cleaner than what it is today, will they be willing to make the sacrifices that will have to be made to insure our planet survives?

As we carried latrine parts up the trail we were occasionally passed by canoeists going the other way. Some had the hang-dog expression of our young acquaintance at the end of the portage, but a smaller proportion had a smile and a cheer in their voice as they passed.

I don't think it had much to do with whether they had ever been on a canoe trip before or not. Some people are better prepared mentally to face such a challenge. Indeed, perhaps they enjoy it so much because they enjoy challenges, or, at the other end of the scale, do not perceive it as a challenge, and not seeing it as such, find no toil in it.

Two young women, teenagers with a youth group, were resting along the portage. It was their task to move a canoe, normally a one person job, to the other end of the portage. As they rested they made the usual remarks about the Horse's length and difficulty but this time I could sense excitement and adventure in their voices. Though they had never faced a challenge such as this, because they were daring and open, they were finding great satisfaction in this simple, though arduous endeavor.

I paused to rest as well and to pick some of the abundant blueberries. They were curious about our job and thought it was "neat" that we were a married couple working together. Gypsy, as always, made quick friends. I told them a little bit about the history of this portage and saw sparks of interest in their eyes. They were from the Twin Cities and this was their first canoe trip. While both were enjoying it, one was especially thrilled, remarking she didn't wish to go home.

The blueberries gave us all a quick boost in energy. They needed a hand getting the canoe up and I showed them what I thought was the best way. Disappearing gingerly down the portage, one trailing the other to take over when the canoe carrier got tired, their girlish voices giggled away into the underbrush.

There isn't much difference between a portage and any other task and the high spirits of these young women will serve them well if they can maintain them through the rest of life's difficult crossings.

Because we have quit dreading portages, Mary Jo and I have begun to enjoy a new dimension in our travels. Taking a portage at the pace that suits it allows us to look around and to examine this other half of the canoe country. The Horse Portage this summer has been a good spot to see grouse. They always seem to be near the last rocky ridge near the west end of the portage, also a good spot for blueberries. Do grouse eat blueberries? I had never thought of it before but Gypsy has flushed this family of six a number of times now and each time they have been in the vicinity of the berry bushes. The first time we saw them the young grouse were no bigger than fluffy robins, and when the dog startled them from their feeding, fluttered upward in a most uncertain fashion and in a very irregular path. Mother simply leapt with a thundering rush to a low limb of a jack pine, just out of Gypsy's reach. She sat long necked and ruffled, teasing Gypsy while the little ones crept or flew away. Now the young ones are the size of quail and they flush and fly strongly, if not yet with grace.

Portages are full of the sights and smells that escape you while on the water. There is the luxurious smell of pine on a hot summer day, the sap oozing from the trees. Was there ever a sweeter perfume? How many golden paths have we trod, carpeted with the spent needles of the pines, a narrow, twisting trail beneath the roof of forest? Where does this path lead? What will you find around the bend? These are the joys and questions of every portage.

Sometimes you will find a grouse strutting in the trail, or a windfall that needs to be surmounted. There are the inevitable mud holes that must be trod gingerly lest voyageur, pack and canoe go ass-over-tea-kettle into the brush. What of moose? Have you ever seen one on a portage or have you, after going across with the first load, returned for another pack only to find moose tracks in the footprints you left only moments before? How could you have walked right past him?

I like the parts of portages that squeeze through dark cedar groves, low areas full of club moss, hummocks of sphagnum and orangish mushrooms. Cool in these dark places, you can see where the scuffing of other feet have left the cedar roots red in the trail. Many times, since these low areas are usually near watercourses, you will see bright yellow marsh marigolds winking at you through the underbrush or catch the sweet scent of wild mint. What canoe tripper does not revel at the sight of blue water through the trees, the sign that the portage has come to an end? What a joy such a simple sight can be and even those who find pleasure in portaging find even more joy in stopping.

We have seen many people on the Horse Portage and others. Over the years I have made a carry with quite a few different friends. More so than paddling, even in high winds or down rapids, a long portage, especially with a little muck and many mosquitoes, can help you judge someone's character.

For me, give me fellow voyageurs who carry with a smile and a tune, or at the very least, shoulder their share of the load and complete the task without complaining. I admire those who make a trip in an orderly fashion, all things lashed into the canoe or stowed neatly in their Duluth packs. These are the same people who will approach life in an organized manner, be capable of handling a job well and can be counted upon if you need them.

And if they also stop once or twice to admire the flowers or pick a few blueberries, all the better. They'll probably find I'll be there waiting for them.

But today we dared not tarry too long. We must make a trade-off between pleasure and labor or we will dig latrine holes well into the evening.

I dropped part of my load at the side trail leading to the campsite. It would mark the spot to turn for Mary Jo. While I waited for her I checked the campsite and found it empty. Gypsy and I gravitated to the black, blue and white waters of the Basswood River, finally stepping into shallow water to cool our feet. We both drank deeply.

I felt no need for a Coke. This portage had been its own reward and if I had needed any other, this slick rapids before us was enough. An alien environment? How could this be? I watched the waters sweep to the west, shining in the heat of a July afternoon, and wondered about the future.

Planned on leaving cabin early for Jackfish Lake. Rain and then a radio warning from Ely of severe thunderstorms and high winds caused us to stay put. When the weather cleared we departed.

Paddled through Wednesday Bay to its southern end. The trip into Jackfish Lake reminded me, in its loneliness, of the Quetico. The lakes here are beautiful but the route challenging because of blowdowns and low water levels.

With the passing of the storm and the coming of the sun, the entire forest glittered with wetness.

• ESCAPE TO JACKFISH LAKE •

Table Rock campsite was empty, as had been all the sites on Crooked from the cabin. We did pass many canoeists on the water though, most being campers we had talked to a few days prior as they were heading in. Their trips were over now and most seemed unhappy at having to leave. I can't blame them.

We turned south at Table Rock and followed the bay to its shallow terminus. I knew as soon as we landed at the portage to Wabason Lake that we had found what we were looking for. The landing, somewhat muddy, showed no sign of human passage and the few rocks hidden near the shallow landing were unmarked with aluminum. Obviously this was a place seldom visited.

This one hundred and twenty rod portage ran nearly straight and slightly uphill, carved through a valley fairly steep in spots. Mud holes on the portage also had no human boot prints and instead were pock marked with moose tracks.

They reminded me of the time I had almost gotten a camper angry when I answered sarcastically her remark about a muddy spot on the Horse Portage.

"The portage was really muddy today," she said with obvious disdain. I got the feeling she was inferring it was our duty to keep them dry.

"You mean that spot about halfway down the portage, beneath the big pines?" I replied.

"That's the one."

"Oh, that's good," I came back, matter-of-factly, "I haven't been able to get back to water it for quite a few days. I was worried it may have dried out."

I felt bad later for being such a smart aleck, but what did this woman expect in the wilderness? It was beyond me.

This portage was serene. Since the thunderstorms had passed earlier it had not had a chance to dry out and we both got wet to the waist pushing through the leafy alder saplings. Gypsy rooted around the portage edges, always hunting. At one point she grew excited and worked back and forth, pulled by her nose. I expected a grouse to flush momentarily but soon the scent must have grown cold for she wandered back to my side.

When we crested a rise the portage dropped to Wabason Lake and the water shined brilliantly in the sunlight. That always welcomed glimpse of blue, framed by the dark forest, that sudden sense of openness and space, that feeling of accomplishment that comes at the end of a portage is something that I've tried many times to capture on film. It never comes for when the photos arrive from the lab there are just pictures of trees and water. Good photographs evoke emotion but I have seen none that can impart the sense of joy, relief and adventure of a portage's end.

The lake was narrow here and banked to the west by rock cliffs, wet and dark. I wondered if we might find pictographs there. I set the canoe down gently, dropped my pack and went back to help Mary Jo with the remaining bundles of tools and gear.

Heading back I realized just how straight this portage was and how wide it had once been. True, alders and balsams constricted the trail but these are fast growing trees that are the first to encroach on logging roads and abandoned trails. I wondered out loud as Mary Jo and I

150

walked back with the last load if this had not been a logging trail at one time, used to snake the timber out of this area down to Crooked Lake. The high hills of the surrounding country would have forced a northerly route for the lumberjacks.

There were very few large pines to be seen anywhere near by and I felt as though my surmise must be correct. Surely the white and red pines from these hills had flowed down this portage.

I took the brush snips out of the tool bag and as I went, clipped some of the alder from the trail, Mary Jo stopping to pick it up to toss it far back in the forest.

Wabason was a very attractive lake, though small. The weather had cleared completely now and the day had grown quite warm. The lake absorbed the blue of the sky and glinted at the crest of each ripple. Drops of water clung to the boughs of every tree. Today the world was made of dripping diamonds and liquid velvet.

I looked longingly down at the fishing rods lashed to the gunwales. I hadn't had nearly as much time to fish this summer as I would have liked, our work days often ten hours long. There was little light or energy left for the fishing I loved when dinner was done. Still, I could not help but wonder what kind of fish, if any, swam in the dark waters of this seldom visited lake. I vowed silently that some day I would return to give fishing a try here.

The next portage was short but rough and wound up a sometimes steep and jack pine choked slope. Strong winds had come here sometime in the past year or two and the gnarled jack pines had been tossed about like straws. Most could be stepped over but a few had to be bypassed. In the open areas the sun shone hotly and sweat poured down from beneath my floppy felt hat, ran down the inside of my glasses and dripped from my nose. It was salty tasting. Horse flies drone annoyingly around my ears and Gypsy repeatedly snapped at those who tormented her, eating a good many.

At last the short portage ended, dropping sharply to a rock ledge a few feet above a creek that flows north to Thursday Bay and south to Jackfish Lake. I could see we would have much difficulty in negotiating this stream for the water was very low and the stream bed clogged with boulders. We'd worry about that, however, after clearing some of the deadfalls on the portage. I set the wood-canvas canoe down in some bushes to keep it from sliding down the hill while we worked on the trail.

It was then that I spotted a mess of white, shining shards on a rock near the river and cursed to myself. I thought I was seeing yet another pile of debris left by thoughtless campers and was angered to find them back here away from the main travel routes. I climbed down to the pile and stooped to inspect it.

I was both relieved and chagrinned at my reaction for here was not the sign of a passing camper but the droppings of two or three otters. The reflective, white bits I had spotted were not trash but crayfish shells, a favorite food of otters. The piles were obviously scat and I cringed at the thought of those sharp shells passing through one's system. Lordy, that must hurt!

The rangers who had trained us had also warned us that we would go through three phases this summer. At first we would be stunned at some of the messes we'd see or violations we'd witness, followed by a period of anger. Finally we'd come to a point of sad acceptance, not any happier to see what we'd find, but able to accept it, clean it up and go about our business without it ruining our day.

I have to admit that we'd not reached that last stage and I had been angry at myself for being so suspicious at times. This pile of shells was a perfect example. Though they were totally natural, I instantly judged it from a distance, assuming someone had left yet another mess for us to clean up. Instead of reading it as a sign that there might be playful otters near, I let it rouse my bile.

It was at this point I believe I finally reached that final stage. Anger was impeding our enjoyment of this summer and we decided then, while talking over my reaction to this incident, that we would try to rule our emotions, lest they ruin our adventure.

Although Jackfish Lake lay invitingly within sight, at the end of the long rocky stream, it was obviously going to take some time to get there. We loaded the canoe and ferried it west across the creek and south as far as we could go. The water was so shallow, and the fallen logs and rocks so numerous, that we soon realized there was no way we'd be able to paddle to the lake. On the west bank we found a place to land and while I balanced precariously on rocks, I handed Mary Jo all but one of the packs.

While Mary Jo held the canoe I removed my boots, put on sneakers and rolled up my pants. The plan was to paddle the nearly empty canoe as far as I could, hoping it would float over what it had not when loaded. If that failed, I'd just jump out and pull it along. Mary Jo would begin portaging our gear along the west shore (the east side was too steep and rocky) and I'd return after reaching the lake to help her.

At first the going was slow but as I knelt in the canoe I felt happy. Here was a wild place, unkempt, the way the entire canoe country should be. I could have just as easily been an Indian exploring this place for the first time and I reveled in the joy of it. No trodden portages, no easy trail, this little bit of difficult to travel creek was just the challenge I needed to bring out the explorer in me. I began to whistle a song from memory and found the tune was En Roulant Ma Boule, one of they happy songs of the voyageurs.

It was no wonder they were so happy. Although the work was hard and they suffered because of poor food, primitive equipment and long hours, they were buoyed up by the excitement of the ever changing panorama around them. When there is something new to see around every bend, when the horizon is never the same from sunset to sunset, who could long be sad?

The contrast of this quiet backwater of the canoe country with the busy border route just two miles to the north was stark. One could experience here what they had come to the wilderness for; challenge, solitude and that infinitely valuable sense that what you are seeing, few if any have witnessed before.

This sense of exploration is important to me, as I believe it is for many others. Deep in the recesses of our ancestral memory, or perhaps woven into the genetic code of species' helix, is the key to this need. Our race has ever been wanderers, always pushing the boundaries of the unknown. It is as if blank spots on maps were magnets or an irritant, a deep rooted need to know what may lay hidden there. I know I am not alone when I say I can spend entire winter evenings pouring over the yellow and blue maps of the canoe country or charts of the Canadian wilds, imagining what it would be like to follow this river or explore the shores of that winding lake. I am never so happy as when those musings become real.

When the water became too shallow to float the canoe with even just my weight in it, I climbed out and waded, pulling and pushing the canoe down the rocky channel. The water was warm and felt very refreshing after the sweaty portage and I looked forward to making camp and a swim.

Mary Jo was halfway to the lake by time I beached the canoe and I went back to help her. As usual, she had attempted to carry too much and I relieved her of half her load. I have never met a better portager than Mary Jo, man or woman. What she lacks in strength she makes up in determination and a willingness to go to her limits, then a bit beyond. Severely injured in a car accident six years before, she was told she may never walk again. If her doctors could see her carry two packs, one in front and one on her back, a canoe paddle in each hand and life jackets heaped on top the pack in back, they would be amazed. I often am.

One more trip with the gear and we were ready to load the canoe and push off. I pushed the canoe to a deep spot where it would float with a load and stood in the water while Mary Jo handed the packs to me. All was ready for departure when I looked into the clear shallows to my left and spotted something unusual.

Three ox or horse yokes lay in the water, the wood grey with age and the chains rusted. I had been right, this had been a logging route. Even on this hot summer afternoon I could picture the cold winter days these yokes had been used, the steam rolling off the horse's backs and their dragon breath driven into the subzero air as they strained to pull their load of pine. When there was no more pine left to sleigh, the yokes were left behind on the frozen creek. Now they lay on the bottom decaying and so nature will reclaim even these.

A good wind had sprung up from the west and as we embarked onto Jackfish Lake it felt good, drying quickly my soggy shoes and pants and driving away the merciless horse flies.

Jackfish Lake was a marvel, at least to my eyes. After seeing the same shores of Crooked Lake and Basswood River for so many days, an unexplored lake was just the change of pace I needed. This lake looks as though it is overfull, brimming up to the edge and likely to spill over. Although the lake was shallow and rocky, and some large hills loomed both east and west, it seemed as if we had reached the height of land. In reality we had been climbing all the way from Wednesday Bay and with Jackfish's rubbly shores and rocky islands it had the feel of a high mountain lake.

And it was quiet and empty, a place we could be alone. I would be very surprised if we encountered anyone in here. I knew no one had gone before us recently on the portages we had just used and the route from the west through a chain of tiny lakes and longer portages was even less likely to be traveled.

We rode the quartering wind down the east shore, past two tiny islands and into the open lake. Our map showed a campsite near the end of a point and we headed for it. Facing the open lake and with a bay to the southeast, we hoped we would be treated to both sunsets and sunrises, an uncommon occurrence and one that was important to us.

When we came to the campsite it was empty and looked clean and inviting from the water, the shoreline strewn with boulders and the banks heavy with jack pine. I quickly looked for a good landing for the day was getting late and we wanted to make camp before taking a swim in Jackfish's clear, warm waters.

While we had traveled only seven or eight miles this day we had actually come much further. We had left the busy border route behind with its crowds and the problems they create for us. We had also left behind on a hot portage, near a pile of crayfish shells, our anger. I had waded a river and heard the song of a voyageur come from my own breast, feeling very much the role. We had seen the remains of the logging era, had read their passing in the alder portage and found their debris on the creek bottom.

We only wanted now to make a tight camp, take a refreshing swim, build a fire and cook dinner. Sunset would be the stage lights and a campfire the floor show. We had found on Jackfish the ancient wilderness again. We were going to enjoy every minute of it.

Another warm, utterly gorgeous day.

Checked portages west out of Jackfish Lake. Portage to Maingan Lake is primitive but passable. Water low in creek to Maingan making it difficult to get to the lake. Walked the portage to Pakwene Lake.

Portage to Sauna Lake hard to find. It begins twenty yards beyond floating bog on west end of bay on Jackfish. Moose have kept this portage well traveled.

All the lakes were lonely and serene. There are some magnificent pines in this area, especially near Maingan Lake.

Did only a minimum of trail maintenance on all portages.

◆ ALONE ◆

We are alone, at last. There is very little evidence that anyone has camped in either of the two sites on Jackfish Lake. One sure method of determining site use is to inspect the bottom of the latrine holes. Not a particularly pleasant job in busy sites but here they were just holes in the ground with signs of little use. The camp we made home has been used only once this year and the other site, nearer the portage, had not been used at all.

Speaking of latrines, I would not have wished to have been sitting on the one in our site during the last thunderstorm. A huge spruce a few yards to the east had been struck by lightning. Spiraling from top to bottom was a naked gash of white spruce flesh and from it were blown chunks of the tree, some pieces landing fifty yards away. One of the tree's roots ran to the latrine and along the ground above this root was a deep furrow rent in the earth. It passed right beneath the rear of the latrine.

Had you been sitting on this wooden box when the lightning hit you may have been the first canoeist on the moon.

We inspected all the portages leading west from this gorgeous lake and found that they were little used. I read telltale signs that the portages coming from Niki Lake had been used within the last week by one party but other than that no one has been this way. I found these portages delightful in their primitiveness; a little brushy and unworn, flowers and blueberries growing along many stretches. They remind me of Quetico portages which are rarely as maintained as are those in the BWCAW. This is good, for a wilderness should be challenging and signs, canoe rests and graveled paths have no place here. If you do not like muddy feet or hard work, go to a state park.

Actually, the portage to Sauna Lake, once we found its entrance which was hidden beyond a swath of floating muskeg, was well traveled, but not by man. Kept quite clear by the comings and goings of many moose, we opted to do no maintenance, feeling we could not improve upon their work.

We did not work hard today. The little bit of clearing we did along the portages took only minutes but I do not feel the USFS has been cheated out of their eight dollars in pay. We make up for it on other days.

I wanted to explore today, as did Mary Jo, and this secluded lake offered all that we could wish. Besides Jackfish Lake we were able to become familiar, only formally I'm afraid, with Pakwene, Maingan and Sauna Lakes. Someday maybe we'll know them more intimately. Each was lovely and lonely and I had the feeling we were intruding upon their privacy.

We also climbed a high ridge to the east of the campsite and found amongst the rows of spreading junipers, blueberries in profusion. An hour was spent picking berries, sitting on our haunches. Our kettles never got full, however, for neither of us could much resist the blue splendor of them rolling in the bottom of a blackened pot. Just about the time we'd have enough to actually do something with, like making blueberry bannock, a hand would dip in and scoop up a mouthful.

Almost synonymous with the north, blueberries were very important to the native peoples who lived here providing a critical source of sustenance. While they are not critical to my diet, I find them no less

important to me for while my body does not require their tart flesh, my soul does. What is July in the canoe country without blueberries? Can anyone who has ever paddled here then look at a blueberry, even the sorry excuses in the supermarket, without recalling a perfect summer day, sun on your back and pine in the air, and a kettle or cup full of their richness?

When I was a child on early trips I recall my poor mother who was kept at the griddle most of an hour, flipping blueberry pancakes for our family. When I see blueberries, this is what first comes to my mind, not so much because the pancakes were so important to my growth, but those first trips were.

Jackfish are also synonymous with the north, both the name and the creature. Found more often in Canada than in the states, the name jackfish denotes the common northern pike. Besides Jackfish Lake there is the nearby Jackfish Bay on Basswood Lake and I have seen this name spattered all across maps of the north country. Jackfish seems to have a negative connotation, probably because small northern pike are a nuisance to fishermen with their voracious feeding and sharp teeth which regularly shear lures from lines. But as the blueberry has been important to many a hungry traveler in the north, so has the jackfish for no fish is quite as easy to catch (small ones, anyway) or has such a wide territory. If a lake supports no other game fish, chances are there will be a least a few jackfish, which is the case here.

We fished for a while today and found that the only fish in this lake are small northerns and perch, which goes a long way towards explaining why it is seldom visited, as well as its name. It is a strange thing, but many canoeists, even those who are not serious fishermen, congregate on those lakes that have good fishing even if they plan on fishing very little. I suppose hope springs eternal. This lack of fish here I feel is a small price to pay for the solitude we have found.

It is interesting to note that this chain of lakes is in the Tick Lake Primitive Management Area, a ridiculous concept of the USFS that calls for setting aside a handful of off-the-beaten-path sections of the BWCAW for minimum maintenance. By special permit parties can enter these PMAs, one group at a time, and find a Quetico-like ex-

perience of solitude. Once the present campsite facilities, such as latrines and firegrates, have deteriorated or need repair, they will be
removed. Campers can then choose a site of their liking, responsible
for building fires in safe spots and taking care of their own body wastes.
This concept itself is not bad, for it works most of the time in the
Quetico. What is a staggering thought is that one needs to create
"primitive" areas within a federally designated wilderness.

Better they should manage the whole BWCAW as a primitive management area by reducing the total number of permits and cutting
party size down to six. There would be far less crowding, less or no
need for replacing latrines and the smaller party size would have less
impact on other visitors and the land itself. There is no good reason
why these measures are not implemented except, of course, there
would be much wailing and gnashing of teeth by those who make
money from the canoe country's visitors. Still, the canoe country de-
serves to be treated more kindly and managed for what is best for it
and not for the area business interests.

Recreation is no different than any other use of a natural resource.
You can only use it so much before you wear it out or deplete it.
Wilderness without solitude is not wilderness.

I have often wondered why the loggers left some of the large pines
that remain yet today. At the west end of the portage to Maingan
Lake is a small stand of huge white pines and one of them was so
large that Mary Jo and I could not touch each other's hands when
we encircled it. Were they left for seed? As landmarks? Perhaps they
were just too difficult to get to and did not warrant the expense. I'm
just grateful they left a few. I can not stand beneath one and not
wonder what it would have been like to stroll beneath many.

We ended the day with another swim; the lake's waters are so warm.
As we dried in the sun an osprey appeared to the west, cruising effortlessly along the shore, watching for fish in Jackfish's shallow
waters. Perhaps he's a better fisherman than I for surely an osprey
must know the best spots and would not come to Jackfish if he did
not expect fish for dinner.

The osprey disappeared down the shore and I never knew if he
found what he was looking for. I hoped he did, for we had, although

our needs were somewhat different. We could do without fish tonight, but both the bird and the volunteer rangers had a similar need for quiet places. Even if Jackfish Lake could not satisfy an osprey's hunger, it had appeased ours.

A rainy morning, complete with an eerie fog that shrouded the islands to our north in grey cloaks. When the sun finally appeared this afternoon and burned hotly, the atmosphere felt like that in a sauna.

Talked to Elkins during morning call. He wants us to meet with Jim Hinds when we go out to resupply.

Replaced latrine in site below cabin taking advantage of its rare, unoccupied state. Many groups passing through the area.

✦ HALIEUTICS ✦

Mary Jo had insisted in hauling it along, although it was redundant. No one needs two calendars. One was for our wall, however, and was large enough so that we could pencil in our work schedule and departure dates. This one, though, was was a desk calendar and each day was a separate leaf. Dictionary-like, it was designed to teach and entertain and we would make a game of it every day as it taught us a new word. Some were so obscure as to be unrememberable. Today it contained a word I liked, a word I wrote down in my journal: halieutics.

Defined as the art or practice of fishing, halieutics (hal-ee-yut-iks) was a word I thought could be helpful to me. As an outdoor writer I frequently pen articles on fishing. One more word to help describe it would be a useful addition to the overworked fishing and angling. Perhaps the real reason I chose to remember this word, however, is that like most brothers and sisters of the angle, I kept a special, though cluttered, spot in my heart for anything that was related to fishing.

I had imagined we would have much time to fish this summer, a mistaken concept shared with those friends and relatives back home who believed that we were spending the majority of our time here doing just that. Although I love to fish, we have found that after hours on the water paddling to and fro, and more hours cleaning campsites or digging latrines, it is a rare day we have the chance or energy to unstrap the fishing rods from where they are always lashed to the gunwales of the canoe. It is my optimism only that has kept them handy much of the summer.

The truth is, we have managed to retrieve them a few times and spend a lunch hour or quiet evening probing the river or lake for an unwary fish. These have been special times for in the midst of one of the canoe country's most fertile fisheries, my fishing addiction has been sorely tempted daily and the chance to scratch this itch thoroughly is relished.

We have found a reef near the cabin where the walleyes school and though they have not been large, they are of the perfect size for a meal. This is the double pleasure of fishing; both catching and consuming. While we practice catch and release angling most of the time, there is great satisfaction in producing the main course for your own meal.

Similarly, we have learned a few good spots for smallmouth bass and an otherwise calm evening or two has been shattered by the spray tossing antics of this fiesty fish. Filleted and skinned, smallmouth from these cool waters are nearly as delectable as walleye.

There are mighty northern pike nearby as well. I had my heart forced into my throat as I watched one rush my lure while fishing below the falls. This pike was nearly four feet long and could have easily broken twenty pounds but I will never know. Stopping just short of the plug, he paused briefly and then darted away into the quick currents, leaving me only with an imprint in my mind of its green-gold form and gaping maw. If they grew any bigger I'd quit swimming.

"The wildness and adventure that are in fishing still recommend it to me," said Thoreau of his quest for perch and pike in Walden Pond. And so it does to me.

While there is great thrill in actually playing a fish, the real adventure for me is just in locating them. There, beneath the rocking canoe, is an entire world almost wholly separate from ours, in which lives are spent to which we are not privy. To find a fish then, and bring it to the surface, even for just a glimpse, is to open a window into that world and let us see its citizens. To actually be able to handle a fish is almost too much joy, to see the wonder of its form and marvel at its function. Everything about them is so alien.

It is common that most people who have strong emotions about killing and eating a mammal or bird have little compunction when contemplating killing a fish. It may be that because fish are cold blooded we feel less kinship with them.

Have you ever held a fish in your hands and watched its eyes? Look carefully. Those cold eyes seem without reason and yet they are invariably looking down, toward the water from which they came. They are aware and know which way safety lies. To deny them the fact that they are cognizant is to lower our own humanity.

Which does not mean that one should never kill a fish. They eat and so must we and we are as much a part of that life cycle as are the eagles and osprey that also prey upon fish. But I have come to respect them more now that I am able to look them in the eye.

Fishing, especially in the canoe country where it approaches the simplicity of the first fishers, has one more thing to recommend it. Besides the adventure, the possibility of a meal and a glimpse into a secret world, it is a quiet and contemplative pastime. I will come away from fishing happy if I caught just one perceptive thought, let alone a fish, and a full stringer to me is not one laden with dead and dying fish. It also teaches something about leisure and patience, two uncommon skills these days, for you can not make a fish bite if it is not so inclined. By virtue of sitting and holding a fishing rod, as opposed to merely sitting, an angler is deemed by his contemporaries as patient and resourceful whereas the sitter is only lazy.

Any opportunity I can secure that allows me to bask in both sun and thought without being labeled indolent is one that soon becomes habitual.

If you will excuse me now, I think I'll go halieuticing.

Went up the Basswood River intending to replace a latrine that was on the work list but found it in good shape. Instead we used the latrine we had brought with to replace one in another site.

Broke up two illegal campsites, one just west of the narrows below Wheelbarrow Falls and yet another one on the U.S. portage, Lower Basswood Falls.

Near Wheelbarrow Falls we met a party whose group leader had suffered a spill on a portage and had gashed his knee severely. We gave what aid we could and radioed Ely with instructions to have someone pick them up at the nearest road.

A grey day with drizzle, but no high winds or hard rain, clearing by late afternoon.

• BUGLING MOOSE •

On a point just east of the cabin is campsite #12. It is a nice site with a panoramic view up and down the Basswood River. Pausing from our work, we stopped to chat with a family of canoeists staying in this site.

We were tired and in no hurry. From where we floated we could see the late afternoon sun dropping into the notch in the west that was the falls. After the usual introductions and questions, we settled back in a more relaxed conversation with the family's father. With a lowered voice he began to confide in us some information he felt important.

"You know that campsite in the bay behind us?" he asked.

I replied that we were familiar with it.

"Well someone back there has a motor. Sounds like a generator to me. I thought motors were illegal here."

Yes, I replied, motors in this part of the BWCAW are illegal.

"What makes you think they have a motor?" I inquired. "Did you hear the generator running or see electric lights?"

"Well no, that's the hell of it," he continued, "they don't seem to be able to get it to run. But I heard them repeatedly trying to start it last night."

A thought dawned. I began to smile.

"Did it go put-put-Put-PUt-PUT-PUt-Put-put and then fade out, only to happen again in a few minutes?" I probed.

"That's it!" he cried. "That's exactly what we heard. How did you know?"

"Where are you folks from?" I asked.

"Missouri."

"Don't have many ruffed grouse down there, do you?"

"Now wait just a minute," he flustered, "you're not trying to tell me what I heard was a bird!"

"Yes sir," I smiled, "you heard a male ruffed grouse drumming. They do that to attract mates or establish territories. First time I ever heard it I was a boy. I thought it was someone starting a chain saw. My dad straightened me out. Don't feel bad, it really does sound like a small engine starting."

He walked away, chagrined.

Noises in the dark can be a fearsome thing to the city dweller thrust into the wilderness. Having no reference for these sounds from their own experience they begin to interpret them in strange ways, often using information gathered from the worst of Hollywood's movies. We encountered some who explained them in very novel ways.

Another time we were talking with four middle aged adults on the Horse Portage and we inquired how they had enjoyed their trip so far. It was their first visit to the canoe country.

"Oh, just wonderful. Absolutely wonderful," chimed one rolly-polly man in tennis shorts, University of Ohio t-shirt and baseball cap. "Last night, just after sunset we heard the elk bugling. It was beautiful."

I informed him that there were no elk in the canoe country.

"I'm sure they were elk, I've heard them on TV," he protested.

Sorry, I said, explaining that while there had been elk here in the distant past, they haven't existed here for hundreds of years. The only large members of the deer family common in these parts are moose.

"Then it must have been moose bugling," he surmised.

Moose don't bugle, they only grunt, I informed him. Perhaps what they heard were loons.

With a look of incredulity he stared at me. How dumb could this ranger be?

"I know what loons sound like. I've heard them on TV too. This didn't sound like that. It had to be moose bugling."

Try as I might, I couldn't convince him that loons have more than one call and he likely had heard one unfamiliar to him. We left him on the portage and went about our duties.

I wonder how many people in Ohio have heard his story about the haunting beauty of the call of the bugling moose?

The call of the loon is also commonly mistaken for that of the timber wolf although they only bear a superficial resemblance. Not surprisingly, every mistaken account of a wolf howl has been reported as happening at night. Seems the dark must let people's imagination run freely. Loons don't sound scary in the daytime.

One young honeymoon couple we encountered on Crooked Lake near Thursday Bay related their terrifying night surrounded by wolves. Seems they were howling all around them. The young woman appeared particularly frightened while her brave, new husband recounted the story.

"It was really something," he said excitedly, "they were all around us. First we'd hear them that way, to the north, then to the south."

Each direction he pointed was over water. In reply to my inquiry, since I was hoping they really had heard wolves because we were to try to locate summer wolf ranges in our territory, he replied that none of the calls came from the forest behind them. When he was asked to duplicate the sound he heard he did a good job of doing a loon call.

"Could have been loons," I said. The bride's face brightened and relaxed when I pointed that out.

"Doubt it," came back the groom, "sounded like wolves out hunting to me."

I wanted to ask him how many times he'd heard wolves on the hunt, but I didn't. He put his arm around his frightened bride and they stood next to the fire as we paddled away.

Most night sounds, if you know what they are, are not only not ominous but entertaining. I love to hear the "who cooks for you, who cooks for you" of owls in the dead of night. I imagine their stocky forms sitting on some tree limb, silhouetted in the moon light on a web of stark branches, round heads swiveling and the final bob, bob, bobbing as they focus in on a moving object, trying to decide if it is something good to eat.

I once had an owl make a pass at my head as I sat in the dark. Perhaps he spotted my moving head and thought it was a roosting grouse. Fortunately for me he saw his mistake in time and as I threw up my arms at the sound of his gliding wings he veered quickly, wings rowing wildly to gain altitude and change direction.

Sigurd Olson had written about another sound, and friends had related similar experiences to me, but I had always thought the tales had a tinge of fancy to them. Not until it happened to me did I fully believe.

We were camped on the eastern-most site of East Pike Lake. This gash of a lake off the end of the Arrowhead Trail is in the most mountainous, and perhaps some of the most beautiful, country in the BWCAW. I awoke in the middle of the night, as I often do on our first night out. I'm not sure why I do this but I rarely sleep soundly until the second night. Maybe I'm too excited to want to waste time sleeping.

While I lay there on my back I heard tiny scurryings around the tent, followed by the sound of something brushing against nylon. Then more scurrying. Then more of the zippp of brushed nylon.

I lay there confused. For the life of me I could not figure out what it was that I was hearing. Slowly the tent roof grew silvery, translucent as the moon crept from behind a cloud. And then I saw it.

A mouse in silhouette struggled up to the peak of our tent and after running along the top for a short distance, slid down the far side. It

was followed shortly by another. A minute or two went by with rustling in the pine needles and then the two mice chased each other up the side and along the ridgeline of the tent, both sliding down with their feet splayed widely. I thought I heard two tiny little "Wheees!"

A sound that is always thrilling to hear during the night is that of wolves. All the countless nights I have spent in the canoe country I have only heard it rarely after dark, though undoubtedly they called more often while I was deaf in slumber.

On Cirrus Lake in the Quetico we were treated to a long nearby serenade. Across a narrow part of the lake from where we were camped was a bay with high bluffs, the kind of place wolves like to make their summer dens. We were just drifting off to sleep when they began, first a solo singer and then the rest of the chorus taking up the tune. I listened a moment transfixed, unsure if I was hearing what I thought I was hearing.

"Mary Jo!"

"Huh."

"Honey, wake up. Listen. Wolves."

"HUH?"

"Wolves!"

Mary Jo came up from her burrow of down, freeing her head and ears. I sat up to avoid the rustling of nylon so I could hear more clearly. Gypsy trembled against my leg. Her head and ears were up.

For what seemed like a long time the wolves sang, sometimes sounding almost sorrowful and occasionally rising to a crescendo of joined voices that reached peaks so pure they sent shudders down your spine. Never once did they all hit the same note simultaneously and their cacophony was joyous. Then silence would fall and we would settle back into our sleeping bags, convinced the show had ended. Then, with a lone wail, a long quavering note, the symphony would begin again.

When we finally drifted off to sleep, they were still singing. Gypsy, I think, must have stayed awake much longer for she was tired in the morning. I wonder what she was thinking as she listened, what stirred within her?

There are two sounds I don't enjoy hearing during the night. One is the ground shivering thud of a moose. While it has never happened to me I have heard of these ungainly deer tripping over someone's tent or its guylines during the night. The tent, and occupants, are usually the loser.

We have had them pass by very near, but never stumble upon us. Mary Jo once spent a sleepless night when I casually, and unthinkingly, remarked as we made ready for bed that it looked like we may have set our tent up on a moose trail. I didn't think much about the statement, but Mary Jo did—all night.

Who can go to the canoe country without worrying about a visit by the pesky black bear? I can say that the visits we've had have been primarily during the day and if bears have come to our camp at night, it has been rare. Mostly the only sure evidence I have that there is a bear in camp is the threatening rumbling of Gypsy's growl. She once almost went through the tent door in the middle of the night and if I had not sat up quickly and grabbed her tail, no doubt she would have. That bear had to have been very near the tent for her to react that way.

I do not worry too much about bears for I am always careful to hang our food packs well out of reach. So elaborate are some of my contrivances for thwarting raiding bears that I have almost wished one would stop by, just to see if my rigging is effective. We've never lost a pack to a bear yet.

That does not mean, however, that the sound of something rustling in the bushes outside our tent in the dead of night won't give me the willies. It is easy to conjur up images of frothing, ravenous bears dragging screaming campers from their tent as you lay there in the otherwise quiet dark listening to strange noises. I suppose the only real way of getting over that fear is to go camping a lot. After a while night noises are no more worrisome to you than would the slamming of a car door be out on the street as you lay in your bedroom. And knowing that frothing, ravenous black bears are far more fiction than fact, helps. The really dangerous part of your canoe trip is driving to and from it.

Mostly night noises are the noises of peace. They are, collectively, the voice of the wilderness. The soft soughing of pine boughs in the wind. The lapping of waves on the beach. The palaver of owls. Waterfowl wings whistling down the river. The steady, measured breathing of your campmates as they drift into a sound sleep.

There is no peace as fair as that of a canoe country night. The canoe is well up from the water and turned over against the wind. Paddles, lifejackets and tomorrow's kindling are stashed beneath it for protection. The food pack is hung well out of a bear's reach. You can smell the wood smoke in your clothing even though the fire outside has been put out.

The sleeping bag feels good and you pull your arms in out of the cool night air. Tonight you will let no night sounds worry you. You are tired and tomorrow brings new adventure. You will sleep the sleep of a thousand dead men. Is there any sleep so fine as one born of woodland exertion, the sun and wind slowly stripping away tension and energy until the body becomes so relaxed that its own weight drags the mind from the world without to the dreams within?

Finally, a loon, very near to the campsite, sings searchingly and is answered by its mate, far down the lake.

They call serenely for a few moments, first one, then the other, then both at the same time. In that dream state before the precipice of bottomless quiescence, the mind moves to ask one last question. What is it that they are saying?

They are wishing you good night.

Inventoried remaining supplies and packed for trip back to Ely. Squashed all non-burnable trash to pack out.

Gave the campsite below the cabin a thorough sweeping, raking and cleaning between parties. This is the second time we've done this site and we still were able to gather five bushels of debris.

Site #14, the one behind the cabin, is showing signs of heavy use. Soil is becoming compacted, large bare spots worn in grassy areas.

◆ PARADE ◆

You can call something anything you want to, but that doesn't make it so. Take the Boundary Waters Canoe Area Wilderness as an example.

I have wandered over the BWCAW and Quetico for years, seeking solitude and for the most part, finding it. In the BWCAW that solitude was usually found by planning a difficult route to an unpopular spot, one devoid of good fishing or reached after numerous and lengthy portages. In the Quetico that same solitude is found much more easily. But there have always been some places I didn't go, some places I purposely stayed away from, not because they were hard to get to or ugly, but because I feared the crowds. They are usually on the U.S. side of the border.

Today we took the opportunity to clean the campsite below the cabin. It has been occupied every night this summer with the exception of just a couple. We have had to dig a new latrine already even though it was nearly empty when we first arrived. Sweeping and raking the camp today we gathered five bushels of debris, mostly the accumulated wood chips and twigs from the preparations of endless campfires.

The campsite behind the cabin is an equally popular site. A Lutheran youth camp discovered it this summer and have kept it occupied almost constantly with teenagers. Although they never break the law by staying longer than allowed or traveling in parties larger than ten, each party is always the maximum size of ten and they time their arrival and departures so that the party leaving holds the campsite for the party arriving. The heavy tread of ten teenagers for two months have worn the campsite seriously. Compound that with the fact that they often send three parties to the three campsites within earshot of the cabin and the wilderness is sorely tested. It becomes a mockery.

Since they are acting within the letter of the law, if not within the precepts of wilderness ethics, it is certain that the present laws are not sufficient for the land's protection.

Two days ago the traffic through this area was especially heavy and I decided to sit below the falls where I could clearly see both portages and make a count of those passing. A steady, cool wind blew from the north down the rift that is the path to the remainder of Crooked Lake. Atop the ridge near the base of the American falls, the high hogback from which I had first surveyed our territory, I sat on the cold granite, munching blueberries and feeling both the warm sun and chill breeze compete as they caressed me. It was a particularly nice seat for watching a parade. From ten in the morning until noon, one hundred and forty-five (give or take a couple) canoeists passed through. I was amazed. Sadly, many of these people were in large groups. I will never understand why people go to the wilderness in sizeable parties.

I knew why this parade had formed, why these people were here. What I wasn't sure about was if they had found what they were looking for. Was their wilderness trip adversely affected by their contact with so many other visitors? Everyone coming to the wilderness expects solitude; one connotes the other and the two are entwined. To bill something as a "Wilderness" and not deliver solitude is to tell a lie, plain and simple.

It would be easy to make a convincing argument that perhaps we are allowing too many people in too large of groups into this wilderness area. If you do not believe that then I challenge you to sit on

176

a portage at Lower Basswood Falls, Knife Lake, Ogishkemuncie Lake, Seagull Lake, Alton Lake, Ensign Lake or along the Nina Moose River during July or August.

Quetico Provincial Park allows only seventy-five parties, with a maximum party size of nine, into the Canadian half of the canoe country. On the U.S. side, in an area of approximately equal size, four hundred and twenty-seven daily ten person permits can be let. It is no wonder that solitude is easier to find in the Quetico. The sensible thing to do, it would seem, is to readjust the quota system to better reflect what is good for the wilderness.

One can only wonder at where this all is headed. Each year the demand for permits rises. Eventually, if the trend continues unabated, the wilderness will collapse under the weight of campers. More money and more rangers can not help this for the campsites will wear and become ugly and noise will permeate the air regardless. Educating users about less destructive camping practices, although helpful, will not stem the tide for there is a finite amount of people that can use an area, even quiet, respectful people, before it begins to take on the dimensions of playground.

Is this what the terrible and emotional battles for the salvation of the canoe country were all about? Saving it from exploitation by developers, the roar of airplanes and motor boats, the threat of roads, logging and mining was not enough. All parts of the BWCAW ought to be equally quiet, equally clean. If we allow the BWCAW to become just another playground, overrun and run down, we will have failed all those who toiled so long to give it to us preserved in its fatal beauty.

If the campsite wear we have seen is typical of that in the more popular sections of the BWCAW, the long term health of the canoe country appears threatened. For what length of time are we managing the wilderness? Ten years? Twenty? With visible wear occurring in just one summer, what will these sites and portages look like in just fifty more years? We must harbor more foresight than to manage this resource for other than just the short term.

I don't know how many more campers crossed the portage that day. After two hours of sitting and watching the parade the little scrap of paper that contained my tally marks was full. I had seen enough. The cool wind had won out over the warm sun and I stood dizzily on the edge of the cliff, stretching my stiff limbs. As I turned to head back to the cabin I heard voices on the American portage. A group was coming down the trail, the lead man depositing his aluminum canoe with a crash on the rock landing.

I walked back to the cabin, cutting cross country through the woods to skirt the two campsites, contemplating what I had just seen. Amid all the questions only one conclusion stood clear.

Calling someplace a wilderness doesn't make it so.

A clear day with a crisp northwest wind. I thought I could feel autumn approaching at sunrise but summer beat it back by noon.

Left Gun Lake this morning for pick-up at Mudro Lake. Took our time, wandering and exploring along the way. Jim Hinds met us at Mudro Landing about 12:45 to take us into Ely.

Cleaned up at the USFS Service Center before having dinner in Ely and driving home to Duluth.

◆ SIDESHOW ◆

"Are you ready to order, Sir?" asked the young waitress.

"Yes, ma'am. We'll have a large sausage, pepperoni and mushroom pizza and a pitcher of cold beer," I answered enthusiastically.

It was a strange sense, sitting in an air conditioned pizza parlor in Ely after so many days in the woods. Both Mary Jo and I were so clean we squeaked after taking showers at the USFS Service Center on the edge of town. Our canoe rested for the first time in weeks, reposing on top of our truck, basking in the sun. Gypsy was most likely sleeping on the driver's seat, a trick she performs as soon as I vacate it and get out of sight.

It was time to resupply for our last stint at the cabin and we had come down Crooked Lake and exited via Friday Bay. A pleasant day of winding our way down through lily choked Papoose Creek and a chain of little lakes had brought us to Gun Lake and as we debated whether to move further on, a whopping thunderstorm pinned us down. Finding a campsite we pitched the tent during a lull and resigned ourselves to spending the night there, great grey sheets of rain rapping on the tent as we huddled inside. I was dismayed to find it still leaked, even after applying new seam sealant. I was disappointed also in that the weather did not clear enough for us to get out fishing. Gun is a very good walleye and smallmouth lake.

Today, with the weather clear and just enough wind to keep things interesting, we sailed down Fairy, Boot and Fourtown Lakes making good time. We had the luxury of having a full day to paddle a route that would normally only take us a third of that time, and we owled our heads at every special sight, shooting photos and lolligagging. I stopped and inspected a large iron ring and pin driven deep into the canoe country bedrock on a point of Fourtown, an artifact of the days when huge rafts of pine had been secured here. This artifact served to remind me that the BWCAW is a "reclaimed" wilderness. If you look carefully during your explorations you will find the signs of railroads, the tote roads and camps of loggers, the occasional trapper's cabins and defunct resorts, all since removed or crumbled. On the Canadian point of land that sweeps down into the heart of Crooked Lake, spanning the width of the distance between Friday and Thursday Bays, there is even an old automobile. I have not heard how or why it was brought into the wilderness fifty years ago, and can only guess it found its way during a winter across the ice. It is a monument of sorts for it is a reminder of what the canoe country could have become. It is also the ultimate piece of litter we have seen.

As we took a breather behind a point on Fourtown we stopped to chat to a man, who, with his wife and children, was on a four day canoe trip. He noticed the USFS emblem on the canoe and we talked for quite awhile, happy to be able to answer those questions we could. It was still early in the day, early at least if you are on vacation as he was, the sun still watery as it climbed from the east, burning its way through the morning's dampness. With the rest of his family still in the tent he asked us to shore for coffee. We declined, anxious to move on, the long drive back to Duluth later in the day in mind.

"How long you folks been out?" he inquired as we prepared to leave.

"Ah, I'm not sure," I hesitated, "but it's been over three weeks."

The man just about dropped his cup of coffee.

"Hey kids, get out here. I want to show you something! Hurry up!" he shouted into the tent.

180

I turned around quickly, sure that maybe a moose had walked down the shore behind us, or maybe a black bear was ambling along. I could see nothing but the pine islands and points of Fourtown and its dappled blue waters.

"Look here," he said when the mother and two children had rubbed the sleep from their eyes. The little boy stood barefoot, dancing on the pointy pine needles clinging to his feet, a small girl clutched at her mother's pants.

"These people have been out here for almost a month. Can you believe it? Where's my camera?"

The young mother looked at Mary Jo and just shook her head. It wasn't too hard to read her mind.

I knew then what he wanted to show the kids. Us. I was already beginning to feel like a side-show attraction but when he asked us to pose for a photograph, I could hear the circus barker call.

"Step right up. See the amazingly dirty rangers. One whole month without a shower! One whole month without television! Watch them writhe on the ground like a snake, burrow like human gophers as they dig latrines! See them wallow in dirt! No electricity, no running water, no indoor toilet! Watch the mosquitoes suck them dry! How do they do it? Step right up. Hurry now, its only one thin dime, two nickels, one tenth of a dollar bill. Hurry, hurry, hurry!"

We posed quietly, smiling, floating just offshore and then paddled quickly away.

Both Mary Jo and I were cold in the air conditioned restaurant and I had to run out to the truck to retrieve our smelly wool shirts.

When I returned the waitress was setting down our pizza and beer. As I handed Mary Jo her shirt the waitress watched, and, as if she might have gotten a wiff of it, asked us a question.

"Been on a canoe trip?"

"Yep."

"How long were you out?"

I glanced quickly at Mary Jo and winked.

"Oh, about a week."

A long but rewarding day.

Decided to try to do something to cut down on the illegal camping on the Lower Falls island portage. We transplanted numerous trees to the area, pine and balsam, putting them in the spots people were using as tent pads and fire pits. The area looked much better for our labors.

Again autumn appeared in the strong north wind that blew this clear day. Come evening I first heard, then saw, a flock of ringneck ducks swing down the river. How wonderful! With ducks flocking, can fall be far away?

• THE PLANTING •

It came to me in the middle of the night. In the back of my mind I had been trying to conjure up some scheme for discouraging people from camping illegally on the falls portage, a problem that has persisted all summer. No sooner do we clean up the site, remove the blackened fire rings and scatter pine needles to hide all traces than does another group decide that this is a good place to camp.

I had considered live trapping a pile of skunks and releasing them on the island. The odor might be enough to deter illegal camping. The plan had some drawbacks, however, especially for the implementor.

I went to bed tired last night, thinking about the problem. It had been a long day, beginning with the drive back to Ely from Duluth and then another tow trip up Basswood Lake to the narrows where the motor ban begins. As the day grew short and the shadows long, we made our way down the river with our last few weeks' supplies. The wind howled the last half of the day and we had been fortunate it had not raged while we were still on Basswood. Even in the narrow confines of the river, though, we were unable to duck its force and it clutched and pulled us toward the east while we struggled west. With the cabin nearly in sight we had to hide behind an island just west of Wheelbarrow Falls, the river opening here into a shallow expanse that was whipped white by the wind. Finally, with our hats off and heads bowed into the gale we knelt in the canoe, determined to fight through the rolling seas the last mile to the cabin.

Crossing the portage at Lower Basswood Falls we found that yet another party had chosen this place for their temporary home. Judging by the depth of the coals in their fire ring, not ten feet from the base of a giant white pine and directly under its gnarled limbs, they had camped here for some time, most likely arriving about the time we had headed to town.

I'll admit I'm not the fastest thinker and while a solution to this problem had eluded me, it was obvious that merely cleaning up after these groups was not the solution. Just as I was dropping off into a restless sleep last night, a possibility dawned on me. If campers could not find a suitable flat spot for their tents, they may just move on. We would plant trees in all the open areas.

We felt much like foresters or farmers today, tending to tiny pines and balsams. From the surrounding forest we excavated as many of the little trees as we could, transferring the saplings from far back in the woods to the problem area. This topic had come up in our training, sessions that now seemed so very long ago. Most of the discussion centered on placing deadfalls, boulders or other obstructions in crucial areas to discourage use of those sites. Still other lessons involved planting trees and shrubs around campsites to define their shape and cut down on the "rural sprawl" that often leaves campsites too spread out. We would combine the two, using the trees to crowd out the possible tent sites.

Laying the saplings out across the problem site we established where they would best serve our needs. Hopefully, as the young trees grew, the portage would begin to look less and less like a campsite. Carefully we planted each of the trees, all the while taking pains to keep the roots moist and undamaged. Spread in a random pattern in an effort to mimic nature, the hill top began to fill with a miniature forest.

There are logical reasons why the Forest Service insists campers stay only in designated campsites. All official sites have both a latrine and a firegrate, both of which are carefully located to minimize problems. Latrines are placed to both offer privacy and to avoid water pollution and some otherwise ideal campsites are eliminated because they do not meet these criteria. Small islands are a typical case. No matter where a latrine might be placed, it ends up too near to the water to avoid having human waste leach into the lake.

Firegrates are installed not merely as a convenience for campers but to make sure that fires are built only in safe locations. These grates are usually placed on large areas of shelf rock or in mineral soil.

The law is very simple and very clear, written on every permit the Forest Service issues. Visitors to the BWCAW must camp at a site that has both a latrine and a firegrate.

By the time we were done planting the trees, the site looked much improved. Some of the ugly areas had been hidden by our efforts and it looked to me that the many little trees would certainly discourage any further camping on that spot. To do so would involve either camping on the trees or ripping them up, something I hoped that no one would consider doing. It had been a full day of labor, at least nine hours worth, but if it would keep the problem from occurring again, the time would have been well spent.

With the satisfaction of a hard day's labor behind us, the fruits of which were very visible as we turned to admire our new and tiny forest weaving in a steady north wind, we returned to the cabin.

We were glad to be back at the falls and our cabin base but we feel already a touch of sadness. While there are more than two weeks in front of us before we must leave, the end that had seemed so indefinite, so far away at the start of the summer, now draws near. Despite some of the frustrations we have felt dealing with people over the course of our time here, the good has outweighed the bad. No one ever had a more beautiful front yard than us, the finger of Crooked Lake pointing to the magical north. Nor was our back yard easy to match, the brawling blue and white waters of the Basswood River. Parting would be hard.

Finally, I must report that someone had a party in the cabin while we were gone. They left plenty of clues as to who they were though. Judging by the evidence, primarily footprints in the dust of the windowsills and kitchen table, and hundreds of miniature, soft, black footballs, I'd say they were small visitors, had large, translucent pink ears and wore grey fur coats. They must have enjoyed our absence, and free run of the cabin, probably chuckling as they left tiny presents on my bunk and pillow.

They'll have it all to themselves again soon enough.

As per Headquarter's request, made a complete inventory to-day of all maintenance projects needed for cabin and boathouse, including measurements and required materials.

Many, many parties camped in the area, including one illegal group today on the Lower Falls island portage.

⬧OUTLAWS AND LITTLE BOYS⬧

A sturdy rap shook the back door of the cabin. I had been in the process of turning off the Coleman lantern, preparing for bed, and quickly turned the gas back on to the still glowing mantle. The lantern roared back to life. It was 9:30 p.m.

If the lights had been off completely I may have stayed in the dark pretending we were not home. We were in no mood to receive company tonight, tired and disgusted dealing with a group that had camped illegally on the Lower Falls portage. It had been a frustrating day.

This was not the first time campers have come to our door. Over the summer we have received guests, most with pleasure, and were used to giving the cabin and boathouse tour or lending aid. One night a young man came to the cabin with a fish hook buried deeply in his hand. Ugly and swollen from repeated attempts to free the barb, he had given up and was hopefully looking for assistance. I examined the wound and suggested a remedy while Mary Jo calmed his buddy. The injured man's friend looked much worse than he, and as we pushed the barb to the surface and cut it off, enabling us to back the hook out from his palm, I swore his partner was going to faint. He was white as a ghost.

We have also loaned tools and rope as well as needles and thread for mending tents and clothing. I have scrounged up nuts and bolts for fixing traveler's broken canoe yokes and have parted with a couple

187

of old paddles we had found along the way, giving them to those whose paddles have snapped and were foolish enough to travel without a spare. There was even an emergency radio call we placed for a young youth camp guide who had fallen on a portage and gashed his leg. Able to walk yet, he had his charges carry the canoe and gear but needed to have his camp send a truck and meet them at an earlier date. Some visits have been humorous. During the first week we were at the cabin, two young men walked right in after lights out. I met them as they came through the door, startling them. Seems they had grown used to the cabin being unoccupied over the years and were planning on staying in it while fishing the area. I informed them otherwise. It was obvious they were familiar with the place because they had packed in mouse traps which they gave to us to add to our trap line.

One Boy Scout group from Chicago even came up and asked us if they could use our shower! Having never seen a building that did not have running water or electricity (they had spotted our lights through the trees and even after seeing the lanterns up close, they thought they ran on electricity), they simply assumed that this cabin, in the middle of the wilderness, would also have both. Not knowing where their water or power comes from in the city, they had never given these utilities any thought, assuming that if you stuck an outlet in the wall or a faucet over a sink, power and water would miraculously appear.

The rapping repeated itself. I went to the door and opened it, peering into the dark of the night. A small voice piped up.

"Mister Ranger, do you have a scale? I caught a big fish and would like to weigh it," said a boy of about ten years of age.

Again I was tempted to end the visit quickly by informing the boy that I did not have a scale, even though I had a small fisherman's model tucked in my Duluth pack. I was still grumpy from an earlier encounter this evening.

We had spent most of the day working on the cabin and listing needed repairs and only afterwards set out to check on the area campsites. To our dismay we found upon our return to the falls area that someone had put up camp on the island portage again.

As if this were not enough, we discovered they had, while making room for their tents, ripped up the seedlings we had so carefully planted the day before. With no one in the camp, we chose to wait for their return, determined that they should at least be exposed to our wrath for their destructiveness.

It was long after dinner time when they returned and the four men stood sheepishly as I chastised them. Not only had they destroyed almost a full day's labor and many seedlings, these outlaws didn't even have a permit for the BWCAW. Mary Jo stood silent, too angry to even speak, her glare enough to crumble granite.

After removing them from the illegal site we paddled dejectedly back to the cabin. Our faith in the human race was at a very low ebb.

All of which was running through my mind as I stared at the little boy standing in the dark, lit by the checkerboard light through the screen door.

"Just a minute, son, I'll get my scale," I said, turning to rummage through my old Duluth pack.

We walked down to the lake together, the night fine and warm, just the faintest afterglow of sunset outlining the spruce spires on the far shore. The boy's dad was waiting, still sitting in the canoe, one hand clenching the dock. I set the lantern down and introduced myself.

"Well Mikey, we don't want to keep the ranger here all night. Show him your fish."

Mikey went to the edge of the dock and took the stringer from his father. Lifting one end over his head, the fish at the other end came shining from the water. It was a smallmouth bass. A very big smallmouth bass.

"I caught him from our campsite," Mikey grinned, "usin' a worm and bobber. Boy, did he fight!"

I chuckled. There was so much joy and enthusiasm in the boy's face. Smiling, I took the stringer from this little Huck Finn and lowered the fish back into the water while I readied my scale. When the bass was dangling from the scale's hook, I turned it toward the light of the lantern, read its weight and quickly pulled the scale's tape measure to the bass' tail. Six and one-half pounds. Twenty-two inches in length.

And it was as skinny as a rail. I lowered the bass again into the inky lake.

"That's a fine fish, Mikey," I said. "These big ones are usually females and if she had been full of spawn, she might have broken the eight pound state record."

Mikey was on his haunches, hand in the water, petting his fish.

"Well son," said the father, "that's a nice fish. You know we've already had dinner so we can't eat it now, and we're paddling out in the morning. What would do you think we should do with it?"

The boy sat pondering for a moment, his whole countenance a picture of thought, a hand still stroking the big bass fondly.

"Geez Dad, it sure is big. I dunno. I think I'll let it go. Maybe I'll catch it again someday."

The father was all smiles and so was I. There was hope after all. I helped Mikey take his fish gently from the stringer. Both of us holding it in front of the tail, I showed him how to slowly ease it back and forth through the water, forcing life through its gills. In a few moments I felt it pulse strongly in my hand.

"Do you feel it, Mikey? Can you feel she's ready to go?"

His blond mop nodded affirmatively.

"OK. Let go."

Kneeling on the dock we watched as the bass fled the circle of light and disappeared into the depths of Crooked Lake. I hoped the boy felt as good about his actions as I did. Both the father and son thanked me and after handshakes all around, I stood on the little dock and watched them vanish into the black night. When I could no longer see them or even catch the gentle swishing of their paddles, I hoisted the lantern and held it in front of me as I rambled up the trail to the cabin, Gypsy darting in and out of the light.

"What was that all about?" inquired Mary Jo drowsily from her sleeping bag when I had finally wandered in.

"Oh, just a little boy teaching me a lesson," I replied. I climbed into bed and turned out the light.

Paddled to Wednesday Bay into a steady, cool wind to clean and check sites. Occupancy rate near 100% but sites were generally in good shape. After lunch we rode what was then a delightful tailwind the six or so miles back to the cabin, stopping to photograph the pictographs.

Planted more trees this afternoon on Lower Falls island portage to try to discourage groups from camping there illegally.

⬩NEVER THROW STONES AT A MAYMAYGWASHI⬩

No matter how many times we pass the pictographs on the painted rocks, we can't do so without stopping to admire them. Two of the most common questions we field are "where are the pictographs?" and "what do they mean?" I can answer confidently only the first.

The display on the high cliffs of Crooked Lake, just a little over a mile from our cabin and the falls, are some of the finest anywhere. At this place the rock leans forward and out over the river, leaving protected areas that were the canvas of the early artists. This cliff has been known for hundreds of years as the painted rocks, but strangely, not because of the pictographs. It has many vegetable and mineral stains as well as the plentiful lichens of the canoe country so that it is remarkably colored with sizable streaks of red, yellow, white, rust and black. The actual paintings are small and unobtrusive, low along the water and mostly along the southern end of the cliff.

Much is still to be determined about the true nature of these haunting paintings. No doubt, as in the art of our own culture, they were painted for more than just one reason. There is evidence to suggest the more abstract pictographs might be the expressions of dreams as seen by the medicine men of the Midewewin society. Hunting magic, wherein the portrayal of your intended quarry helps to visualize the hoped for outcome of a supply of needed meat, is common throughout the world in primitive cultures and it is quite likely that the Ojibway, or their ancestors, may have practiced similar rituals. Undoubtedly some pictographs are simply historical billboards, marking the passing of some important event.

But there is always an element of magic. The Great Lynx, or Misshepezhiew, can be frequently seen and is recognized by the horned head and long reptilian tail. Legends say that it is the Misshepezhiew that created storms on lakes by thrashing its monstrous tail and formed the shifting currents that capsized canoes in rivers. Many Indians offered gifts of tobacco to the Great Lynx to appease its spirit, especially before undertaking a dangerous, open water crossing or at the top of suspicious rapids. What better place then for an offering to the Misshepezhiew than at the confluence of confusing Crooked Lake and the perilous Basswood River?

Some passerbys have informed us that though they paused to look for the pictographs, accurately describing the right cliffs of Crooked Lake, they could not see them. Perhaps they had expected something too large or too colorful, for the pictographs are small and dark red. Near the water, they are rarely any higher on the cliffs than a person could paint while standing in a canoe. Maybe those who are unable to see the pictographs are not just unobservant but are so civilized that these magic paintings simply are invisible to their eyes.

There is also a small figure here, off by itself, a tiny man-like drawing with arms outstretched. I used to call this little man the "first fisherman" since with the arms wide spread he seems to hold the pose of so many anglers who brag about the one that did, or didn't, get away. I have since learned that this figure, which we have encountered in so many places in the northern lake country, is a Maymaygwashi. The Maymaygwashi is a figure of deep magic, both mysterious and sometimes devious. I once discovered just how devious he could be while canoeing the north part of the Quetico.

The day was a rare one, full of canoe country magic. We could feel this deep magic, feel its rhythms and mysteries as tangibly as though they were rain or wind as we paddled along. Caught up in the spell, I thought of those who had gone this way before us, those aboriginal peoples who had lived in this fair country. The ancients were in tune with those mysteries, understood the lake country's moods and had left sign of their understanding through the pictographs still visible on the cool rocks along dark shores.

We, who venture into this ancient land on occasion only, struggle to read the meaning in these paintings. We laugh at eccentric moose smoking pipes or the funny little men with arms outstretched. In the egocentric way of modern man, we assume we know more than our ancestors, and that they were but children compared to us.

Though we understand so very little about the hidden meanings of these mysteries we are no less affected by them as were those who formed those eloquent paintings. They speak of the elements, of wind and rain. They speak of food and war, of blood and wonder. They speak of man's need for a spirit world. These are things that none of us are separate from and though we might be sheltered by the cocoon of our civilized lives, all these things can, and do, affect us intimately and no less profoundly.

The day was warm and fair, blue skies a velvet backdrop for the few billowing clouds. A steady but manageable wind blew at our backs most of the day and we made wonderful time as we paddled down the lake's length. I kept a fishing lure dragging behind the canoe and we consistently caught fish, finally keeping one medium size walleye for our dinner.

All down the lake's north shore we saw many pictographs. We stopped a few times to wonder at them, to take photographs. More than once we encountered the stick-man Maymaygwashi and I tried to recall what I had learned of him.

I had read that the Maymaygwashi is a mischief maker, the Indian leprechaun. I had also read that the Indians believed these little hairy faced people were fond of fish and often stole them from the Indians' nets, that they could change form and frequently played mischievous tricks. It is said that they could disappear by paddling their canoe into cracks in the cliffs.

Why had these little men come to be painted in just these spots? Was there some significance? Had there been an encounter with the Maymaygwashi nearby? We floated beneath them and wondered awhile before moving on.

We selected a high, jack pine studded island that evening for camp. Though the island was small, it afforded an excellent spot for our tent near its peak with spectacular vistas in three directions. After the busy routine of making camp, and before dinner, we settled down for a sip of brandy and the chance to write in our journals. At one point I glanced up from my writing for a view of the lake and saw a strange sight.

In the open water, about seventy yards from the camp, bobbed a fish on the surface. I thought this a bit out of the ordinary and watched it for a few seconds before returning to my journal. Then it dawned on me. Perhaps our walleye dinner had torn the stringer free.

Racing down to the water's edge I searched the bushes for the stringer. Finding it still fast to the limb, I pulled it from the water. The walleye was gone! What was more confusing was that the cord stringer was still passed through the brass ring. The fish would have had to break its own jaw to have escaped. I thought that hardly likely.

I could see our dinner floating off shore. Sliding the canoe quickly into the water I paddled furiously out to where the fish struggled, tail up. Moving in very quietly so that I would not scare the fish away, I eased my hand over the side of the canoe and as I drifted near the fish, made a move toward the now submerged walleye's tail.

As my hand had approached the tail I saw that something was wrong with the fish's head. Indeed, something was very wrong. Hanging on to what was left of the jaw was a huge snapping turtle, one perhaps of forty pounds. He eyed me malevolently from two feet down.

Fully aware of what those jaws could do to my hand should he decide to strike, I nonetheless was reluctant to give up my fish dinner. Waiting until the snapper let the fish bob to the surface, I made a swift grab the walleye's tail.

A tug of war ensued that I should have no doubt lost had the huge turtle not torn the head from the walleye. I quickly hoisted the remains of the fish into the canoe. In good shape except for the missing head, we would have our walleye dinner after all. I laughed at the turtle and paddled away.

With the weather warm and the fish now dead, it would have to be filleted and cooked before it spoiled. Dinner would come early. I knelt down on the sloping rock shore and began to fillet the fish on a canoe paddle. The sun was starting to drop and I could feel the warmth of the huge orb beat steadily on my back, a breeze cooling the perspiration on the back of my neck. Halfway through the task of cleaning the fish I had a strange feeling that the sun was not the only thing behind me.

Turning quickly I was startled to see the big snapping turtle only a few feet from me, his back out of the water and his head only a few inches from shore. I jumped up and stood between the turtle and the much desired fish. Do snapping turtles ever come out of the water? I was determined not to find out.

I found a large stone and hurled it near the fish thief, forcing his retreat to slightly deeper water. I hurriedly finished my filleting task, (this time facing the water) rinsed the fillets and headed to camp. I scraped the fish remains from the paddle to a rock on the water's edge to see if the turtle would come up and finish them off. If not, I'd return and bury them later.

There seemed something strange about this turtle's conduct. The thought of it pestered me.

The fish dinner allowed me to forget my concerns. A fine, calm evening settled in, just made for a leisurely paddle. Filled with the sounds of dusk and the swishings and swoopings of nighthawks and bats, we hurried the after dinner chores so that we might have time to explore before dark. Leaving the cleaned dinner dishes overturned on a rock to dry, we launched the canoe and drifted into the last light.

In the twilight, Mary Jo asked to be put ashore for a few minutes. We found a likely spot along a dark, spruce shore and I paddled the canoe parallel to the sloping rock. Mary Jo and Gypsy hopped out and disappeared into the bushes. For a moment I sat calmly enjoying the evening.

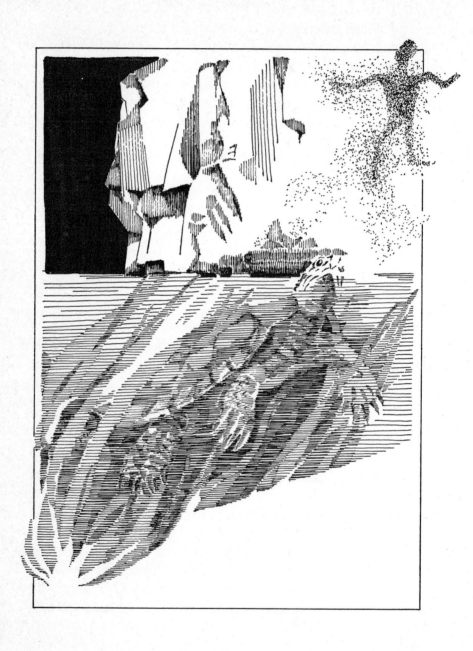

The next thing I knew I was submerged in five feet of water, the canoe floating over my head. I quickly found bottom and stood up, thrusting my head into the air. I looked around, startled, and saw the canoe floating right side up, high and dry, a few feet from where I had let my wife out. Heavy with water soaked clothing, I dragged myself turtle-like onto the rock shelf. By this time Mary Jo had returned, and relieved that I was OK, began to chuckle.

"Did you see the turtle down there?" she asked, laughing.

The turtle! Of course, the turtle! Somehow he was behind this, somehow he had managed to get even. But could a turtle be so scheming? It was then I recalled the pictographs we had seen on this lake today. We had seen so many little men with arms outstretched! I quickly recalled their mischievous ways, their extreme fondness of fish. Whether from wet or wonder, a chill gripped me.

"Well," repeated my wife as she steadied the canoe for her soggy husband to step into, "did you see the turtle?"

"That was not a turtle," I said.

"Oh? What was it?"

"A Maymaygwashi."

"A what?"

"Maymaygwashi. You know. The Indian leprechaun."

My wife chortled in comprehension. "Well of course dear. You should know better than to throw stones at a Maymaygwashi."

"Hmmphh." Indeed.

I have pondered this event in the days that have gone by and have become thoroughly convinced that my surmise was correct. Surely I had met a Maymaygwashi. To me there could be no doubt. And at last I began to understand that those who lived in the canoe country in years past knew well what they were expressing when they painted those pictographs. If I had had some red paint on that canoe trip, I too may have left a Maymaygwashi warning on some rock cliff near where we had matched wits.

Just what had happened near the cliffs of Crooked Lake to be responsible for the appearance of the little stick man on those rocks is unknown. But I feel as though it must have been something that was otherwise unexplainable, and perhaps even humorous. That is the nature of the Maymaygwashi.

If you ever paddle near there, I'd be damn careful.

Cruised up the Basswood River to haul a new latrine to a campsite on the Horse Portage.

Many, many folks today. In the first three miles of river we encountered 24 canoes carrying 54 people. Figured another way that's 8 canoes or 18 people per mile. Either way, it's too many people for a wilderness area.

Were delighted to meet two Quetico volunteer rangers on the river and spent some time chatting with them. On our way back to the cabin this afternoon, as we were launching our canoe at the bottom of the portage around the Chute, we were surprised to see a canoe with no one in it sail down the rapids. We paddled to it quickly and pulled it from the current, holding it for the married couple who had lost it when their rope broke as they lined down the rapids.

• WOLVES •

I was returning across the portage for the second load when I spotted it. There, in the middle of the trail that skirts the rapids known as the "Chute" between Horse and Wheelbarrow portages, lay pale and sere a four inch chunk of what looked like thick, twisted rope.

Of course I knew what it was, that it wasn't rope. I had learned from a ranger one summer years ago while hiking across Isle Royale that what I had been seeing scattered on the high greenstone ridges were wolf droppings. Wolves, eating just about the entire carcass of their kill, also devour the hide. The fur or hair passes through their system and resembles, once dried, the strands of coarse rope.

I toed the droppings gently and seeing that they were completely dry, stooped to pick them up. The hair was a mixture of white and gray, no doubt due to both bleaching by the digestive system of the wolf and from exposure to the elements as it lay on the trail. There was no question, however, as to just what kind of animal the wolf had killed and eaten. As a hunter myself I had inspected this type of hair closely before, the hair of a whitetail deer.

I had no way of knowing just how old these droppings were but I guessed they were from the previous winter. Certainly the wolves would not use this portage during the busy summer but instead had traversed it in the cold, white months when the canoe country once again became theirs. I also guessed that now, during the summer, it would be rare that wolves would be able to catch the fleet footed whitetail but were instead most likely feeding on smaller animals such as the beaver. I wondered about how this deer had met its end.

Whenever I see this telltale sign of a wolf's passing, and the observant will find such clues on portages all across the canoe country, I remember the time three of us came across a fresh wolf kill. We were cross-country skiing in the deep snow country of the Sawbill, south of the midsection of the BWCAW. My wife, a friend and I had just finished a lunch stop and had resumed our trek. We were climbing a gradual incline when we spotted wolf tracks in the snow. The tracks were huge, at least twice the size of those our seventy pound dog Gypsy makes, and in their midst was the spoor of a lone deer.

A short distance up the trail I spotted a bloody patch of hair. Before we skied on I inspected the sign. Here was where the wolves had first caught up with their prey, a prey that must have been fleeing in wild eyed terror. I could picture the scene, hear the almost eerie silence, the only sounds the short gasps of the desperate deer and the panting of the wolves, each of their breaths, predator and prey, pumping white clouds into the sub-zero air. It looked as though a piece had been torn from the back of the deer's haunch in an attempt to hamstring the animal. This bit of hide, perhaps as big as wolf's mouth is wide, lay at the site of their first encounter, dark blood dried where the hair had been torn out by its roots.

I grew excited by the sight. Even in northern Minnesota where wolves still live in fair numbers, it is not typical to stumble across such a fresh kill. No one had skied this trail since the last snowfall

and I knew that if we followed carefully and watched for more signs we might be able to read the history of the struggle.

Within one hundred yards we came upon the site of the kill. In a depression to the right of the ski trail the snow was pounded into a flat circle. In the middle of the circle was all that was left of the deer; scattered hair and what looked like stomach contents. All over the site were many wolf tracks and like planets in orbit around the sun there were six smaller, trampled areas, areas also littered with deer hair and blood. Looking at those orbiting depressions I thought of how the wolves in their excitement must have dismembered the deer, the alpha pair feeding first and then the rest of the pack each pulling off a piece and settling down to eat.

There were no large bones to be seen and I wondered what happened to them. Had they eaten even the skull? The kill was fresh for snow had fallen just the day before. The deer had met its end most likely last night. Could they have so thoroughly consumed and entire deer in such a short span of time?

Leaving the site of the kill through the birch and balsam forest were two sets of wolf tracks, running parallel in the deep snow. I skied down one set to see if they might lead me to some further sign, perhaps some of the large bones. What I saw surprised me.

About thirty yards from the kill site the two sets of tracks converged, the snow disturbed by turmoil. In this depression I found more hair, but it was not the hair of a deer. I picked it up and examined it. No, there was little doubt. It was wolf fur. At this spot two wolves had struggled, perhaps a dominant animal reprimanding a subordinate for making off with a choice part of the kill. I put the fur in my pocket. I skied on a little further. There was no evidence of the bones I had been looking for.

Later I compared that fur to a wolf hide at the U.S. Fish and Wildlife Service office in Duluth. It looked to me that this bunch of fur had been nipped from the feathery area on the backside of a wolf's haunch. Not meant to maim or be fatal, that nip had been delivered to assure that the pack's order would be kept. I thought to myself that the pack leader just might want to keep an eye on this bold youngster.

That wolf fur sits on the bookcase of my office at home and I think of this experience, and of that life and death struggle of which each of us is a part, whenever I pass it.

Though the deer's death was seemingly violent and cruel, it was no more than the consequence of the wolves' being alive. The cycle is endless. Though many of us may never physically take the life of another animal, we are responsible for deaths every day, our very existence dictates it. Even if we were never to eat meat or wear skins or furs, we sacrifice other creatures' lives by building our homes on theirs, by plowing up their meadows to grow our grain and by allowing our cities and suburbs to eat away at their habitat.

I find no shame in being a predator. Who is ill, those who can not face death and the consequences of being alive, preferring to hire the job of making meat to others; or those who have seen death, taken life and know their place in the eternal struggle? Both life and death must be dealt with respectfully and with open eyes. They are two sides of a single coin and you can not spend one without the other.

The sun danced through the leaves, casting fleeting shadows on me as I examined the dry wolf scat. My thoughts were interrupted by a scuffing in the woods and I glanced down the path to my right. Mary Jo and Gypsy came down the portage, my wife struggling with a heavy load of tools and latrine parts, no doubt wondering what in the world was taking me so long in coming back to lend a hand. I rushed up to greet her and take a part of the load, showing her the reason why I had been tardy. I held the wolf droppings down near Gypsy's nose. She sniffed it with mild interest and then, walking over to where I had found it, squatted and left her own message. This was for now, she was saying, her portage, although I felt she may be bragging a bit in her possession.

The Canadian portage ends in a steep, gravelly hill, dropping down to the swift, dark waters of the Basswood River at the very brink of the rapids. We stepped out of the forest into the hot summer sun, glad to drop our load near where I had put the canoe.

After carrying the canoe to the water, I stood boot-top deep, holding the boat parallel to the current. The water was cool on my feet and

I could feel the gravel washing from beneath them as I waited for Mary Jo to hand me the packs. The river looked viscous; thick, powerful and dark.

While we were loading the canoe I glanced up across the river. A whitetail doe and her fawn drifted down to the water's edge on the American side and stopped to drink. When they spotted our movement, ears pricked toward us, heads bobbing to trick us into moving, they turned and melted into the forest, the doe nudging her fawn up the hill. They were the promise that life would go on, that the struggle with their ancient adversary, while fatal to the few, would endure through generations.

We finished loading and pushed off into the current, paddling hard to escape its grasp, heading toward Horse Portage. The day was getting on and we had a latrine to install.

Paddled to Thursday Bay and back, checking and cleaning sites. Ran into two more Quetico volunteer rangers in Wednesday Bay.

Firegrate we installed (the one that had been stolen) in site #33 now has four rungs broken.

We were flagged down by two men that reported a bear had made off with one of their packs. Unfortunately they had kept a little food in a gear pack and instead of dinner, the bear found a pack full of camera gear, their wallets, stove and fishing tackle. They never did find their pack. We scrounged up some old cooking utensils for them to cook and eat with.

Fixed latrine at Table Rock campsite.

A big black bear came to our cabin door this evening and peered at us through the flimsy screen. Gypsy went berserk and the bear backed off. I put the dog on a leash and used her to drive the bruin back into the forest, hoping I could deter it from visiting any of the area campsites.

♦ JACKPINE MIRACLE ♦

A red squirrel busied itself at the top of a jack pine, stuffing, in its frantic way, one more seed from the pine cone into its mouth. Cheeks puffed beyond belief, the seed slipped and fell, tumbling through the boughs and striking the bedrock below.

With a single bounce the seed tumbled off the edge of the cliff along which its parent tree grew and was saved from falling into the water of the narrows at the south end of Wednesday Bay by a small ledge. It lay there some days until a heavy rain came and when the torrent of water that had leached through the shallow soil above reached the bedrock base, it flowed like a small waterfall over the cliff, dislodging the seed.

Once more the seed began to move downward, this time through a diagonal crack in the granite itself. This was not the first time water had followed this route. For eons the crack had grown, widened by the imperceptible wearing of water and the repeated frosts of bitter winters. Its edges worn from centuries of weathering, it was now a few inches wide.

Had the seed fallen in that crack in earlier years it likely would have been flushed into the river to decay. But the seed had been preceded by other debris, and lichens had for many long years been working tenaciously, the entire rock face and crack roughened with their growth. Pine needles and bits of earth had clogged one chink and caribou moss had eked a livelihood out of that meager field for decades.

It was into this moss that the seed fell and wetted by the rain and warmed by the sun it began to germinate, sending shoots through the lacework bed. Twenty feet above the water in a crack on a vertical rock face, it was all it could do for a few years to just retain its grip, buffeted by rains, wind and ice. By the end of its third year it was only two inches tall.

As it grew, the seedling probed the recess of the crack, looking for a foothold on the barren surface. One root shot upwards from where it had fallen, another reached down to the lake and spread-eagle it began to grow, each year increasing its girth and height. Fifteen summers it grew, fifteen winters it shuddered until the tree was four inches through at the butt. Even on the hottest of summer days, and through long droughts, the tree was watered; roots sucking the moisture deep in the recesses of the crack when the rock would sweat.

Ten feet tall, the tree had grown and umbrella of branches, brilliant green clustered needles against the grey rock and blackened lichens. Though there was no soil to feed it, the tree grew straight. It was a tiny miracle in a hard land.

One day a squirrel busied itself in its branches, harvesting the few cones the little tree managed to squeeze out. Stuffing its cheeks frantically, the squirrel dropped one seed.

We paddled to the junction of Friday and Thursday Bay and back today, a circuitous route of some twenty-five miles by the time we had poked into all the odd corners. Checked all campsites and cleaned those in need.

Most campsites are in pretty darn clean condition considering the heavy use they are receiving.

Saw two immature bald eagles soaring in the Wednesday-Thursday Bays area as well as numerous turkey vultures. I have a feeling that today's strong winds were better for soaring on than paddling into.

◆ NAMES ◆

Hunger overtook us at Lunch Rock. I eased the canoe parallel to the granite slope and stepped creakily into six inches of water, turning to steady the canoe for Mary Jo and Gypsy. When both had climbed to shore I placed two paddles, blades to the lake, beneath the canoe, three feet apart. Gently I tugged the canoe sideways onto the paddles, thereby saving unloading all of our gear and also dragging the canvas skin on the abrasive stone. I retrieved the lunch items from a pack and carried them up the lichen covered shelf.

This has become a favorite place for us to rest. Just south of the international border, it lies about a half mile south of the Big Current. A little island, too small to camp on, it sports a crown of a few dwarfed trees and the always present junipers. Because it is so small and open, it is swept clean by winds and rain, leaving it always inviting.

Lunch Rock is not so named on any map. Neither is the Big Current a short distance away. These are places that are named only in the minds of travelers and this rest spot, only in ours. Big Current, so named because of the short rapids between the mainland and a big island north of the point between Wednesday and Thursday Bays, is known by many as such, especially by the fishermen who angle for walleyes at its bottom. It is an unusual occurrence, for one does not often find such a phenomenon as rapids on a lake.

I doubt that anyone who ever frequented this area could forget such a place and it is very likely that since the first peoples came here, the Big Current has been known by that name. I can not be sure, but I would wager that the Sioux, Ojibway and French names for this landmark would translate all the same into English: Big Current.

There are other obvious names for places in our territory; Picture Rock, Lower and Upper Falls and of course, Crooked Lake. All are simple and descriptive and have been used in one language or another for hundreds of years.

Modern trippers call the deceptive rapids below Horse Portage "The Chute", which also is descriptive. Although apparently not dangerous to the casual observer, it has cut a trip short for many paddlers. No rapids with two portages, one on each side, should be taken lightly.

Horse Portage, the mile long trail around the upper falls and rapids of the Basswood River, has been known by many names. Alexander MacKenzie, a great explorer with the North West Company of fur traders, called the Horse Portage the "Portage de Bois Blanc." In 1797 David Thompson, formerly with the Hudson's Bay Company, named this landmark portage the "large Pine Carrying Place." What the Indians called this place has not been recorded.

Table Rock is also fairly descriptive. One would need a good imagination to make its huge granite presence look like a kitchen table but any voyageur, modern or ancient, would have found this slab useful as such. Its name belies its use, not its appearance.

There are strange names too, like Horse Portage and Wheelbarrow Portage. No doubt these retained their names from the types of conveyances used at one time to make passage easier. Or how about Circle Lake which is distinctly square and Frolic Lake which it is anything but to get there?

No lake has been so aptly named as Crooked and to the uninitiated it can be mighty confusing. The first time I ever paddled this massive, contorted lake was on a cloudy, drizzly day. With no sun to guide me, my map and compass came into repeated use. Even when knowing which direction you are heading, there are so many blind bays, points and islands that one can paddle for miles around obstructions just to go a very short distance. Early travelers often made use of an Indian guide to direct them through this piney maze.

I once met a man at The Chute who had been lost for three days on Basswood Lake. He declared he had forgotten his compass at home and when we found out he was heading to the far more confusing Crooked Lake, we grew concerned. I gave him our spare compass. To this day I wonder how he got along.

I have heard that the weekday bays of Crooked Lake are so named for good reason. After spending Monday and Tuesday reaching this lake many have spent one day lost in each bay until finally, on Sunday, they reach Sunday Bay, where the roar of Curtain Falls leads them to the exit. I believe there is much truth to that story.

And we have added our own names, as have the countless other voyageurs who have explored this beautiful region. Our names, however, will never appear on maps or be used by any but ourselves. Named for events in our days, they have become priceless reminders of simple joys.

Otter Point, Lunch Rock, Ringneck Bay, Big Pike Narrows, Walleye Rock, Bird Tree, Burnt Pine Island, Iris Point and Smallmouth Rapids. Each is a place of fond memories, each a piece of this wilderness that recalls what to us was some valued experience. You know you are rich when you can not only name such places but close your eyes and see them, feel them and smell them, even from miles and years away.

I can not go into the woods without each time etching some place of unique beauty into my mind. They all receive some such simple name and I can recall them almost at will. What is even a greater gift is when the memory of one floods back into the channels of my mind, washing with it the very colors, sounds and textures that belongs to it alone. In the dead of silent winter I will be transported to some glaciated spit of rock poking into the promise of a lake I've come to

explore. The gulls will cry overhead, wheeling white against blue. The summer sun heats my browned skin. I can hear the crunching of dry caribou moss beneath my boots, feel the breeze on my cheeks as it passes to whisper the enticements of wilderness in my ears. Every rock is as it was. The waves lap softly as they had. The lace light of sun through pines dances as it did. Do not trouble me with the names of great cities or their streets for I want not to remember them long. I am saving space in my mind for the names of other places, places wild and untamed.

Lunch Rock will be one of those names. Someday, as I sit in a crowded and noisy cafeteria or a stuffy business luncheon, I will close my eyes and conjure up Crooked Lake.

It's not such a difficult trick, if you know the right names.

Mary Jo didn't feel well today; perhaps yesterday's long labors wore her out. While she relaxed I cleaned the boathouse in preparation for our last trip out.

Discovered the most amazing nest in the boathouse logs.

◆ WINTER WRENS ◆

It turns out we are sharing the boathouse with another creature. I stumbled across this when passing the back door and a brown buzz bomb whisked erratically past my ear. Ducking reflexively, I turned to see a small clump of moss, bored neatly with a quarter-sized hole, tucked between two of the wall's logs and the door jamb.

I watched quietly for a few moments and was rewarded by the return of my attacker, a delicate little bird no larger than a deer mouse. It landed in a rush at the top of the steps that lead down from the cabin trail, granite blocks placed there long ago by the boathouse builders. Covered with moss they have become a part of the landscape.

The minuscule bird, which I determined later to be a winter wren, carried the mouse analogy further by darting furtively through the ground cover, its herky-jerky movements almost comical. Apparently annoyed that I remained so near its nest, it eventually flitted off into the forest.

I advanced to examine the nest more closely. Constructed ingeniously of moss and spruce twigs it adhered tenaciously to the hollow in which it had been built. I marveled at the construction because it it seemed to me that the combination of the two materials could have been no accident but the result of much evolutionary trial and error. The little twigs have a rough finish that catch in the many folds of the moss, creating a moldable but adhesive building material. These are the same bare twigs you find sticking to the strands of your woolen sweaters and socks. The effect here was the same.

For some reason I clucked my tongue, perhaps in amazement, the same sound a rider might make to giddy-up his horse. Instantly a pair of bright yellow, gaping mouths appeared at the nest entrance. Grey bundles of down and mostly muzzle, their tufted heads gave them a decidedly Dr. Seuss-like appearance. When they found no food waiting for them they disappeared into the recesses of the nest. I clucked again. Again more yawning maws, but this time there were four of them, all straining to reach the opening. I had accidentally discovered a sound, maybe similar to one made by their mother, that triggered a feeding response. I felt fortunate we had one phrase in common.

I returned to the cabin to retrieve my camera and to tell Mary Jo about what I had found. I almost told her we had visitors but caught my error. It was the birds that were taking callers.

It has been a long time since most of mankind was a resident of the forest. Not being residents we can hardly have visitors. We are all visitors now. Only in sparsely populated regions of the far north, or in the yet unexplored regions of the Amazon jungle, do men still dwell as a part of nature. The burgeoning third world populations are primitive only by the weight of numbers and live more as adversaries to than residents of the land. The developed nations, having subdued the land to their needs, are no longer residents of it, but on it.

This nest was a marvel of nature's architecture, a complex structure woven of two simple materials. About eight inches in length it narrowed to three points, one each at the top, bottom and right side where it pressed into the contours of the logs. The left side was vertical against the straight line of the door jamb. It was a diamond cut in half. Most of the twigs were in a circular pattern, woven around the nest's door which was just above center. The tiny family's home was beautiful and alive, both inside with grey balls of down, mouths and hunger, and outside with the intricate star shaped moss of the canoe country. The moss apparently did not mind being used as a nest for it was green and thriving. It would serve its purpose long enough and when no longer needed, would fall to the forest floor from where it had come. In this respect nature is a better engineer than man.

Is there much difference between a moose trail and a portage? Can you tell who, or what, was the engineer? Both serve the same purpose and are constructed of the same materials. Who shows more sense, the moose who wind their way around some bog, the Indians that portage around a dangerous rapids or the road builder who hauls in fill to level the bog? Sometimes the portage and the moose trail are one and the same and neither the tribe of man nor the tribe of moose much care who uses it. At some point the importance of "getting there" so straightened out man's trails and sped up his traffic that any creature other than man receives a death sentence for its trespass. We became niggardly neighbors.

I spent much time this day, poised with camera and tripod, waiting for the mother wren to return. She would approach within ten yards of the nest and light in a tree to study me, as I was her, and when she determined I was not a threat, would flicker nervously to the nest entrance. Though I never heard her make a sound such as I had, the many gaping mouths would appear as soon as she lit. What she fed them I could not tell, even through the reach of my telephoto lens. But she did so very quickly and was gone in a blur, so fast that it was many attempts before I figured I had captured her on film.

I folded up my tripod and prepared to move on. I had interrupted the important business of feeding too long. Gypsy shot up the steps and trail toward the cabin but I paused briefly at the nest as I passed. I clucked.

Five heads shot up. Five! I chuckled because now I knew why the little wren was so furious in her flight, so rapid in her coming and going. She had to be.

Paddled east to Horse Portage and put a new latrine in at one of the Basswood River campsites.

We met our friends Bill and Terry on the Horse Portage and accompanied them to the cabin. Shortly after our return, Sam arrived. It is good to have friends visiting. Had a wonderful dinner of fresh foods.

Speaking of food, bears have begun to be a problem in the cabin area the last few nights, raiding a couple of camps and stealing food packs. One actually swiped an unwashed dinner pot, took it to the edge of the forest and licked it clean while the campers watched.

◆ STEAK AND POTATOES ◆

It would have been easier to have brought the whole cow and have it walk across the portages. That was my first impression when I saw the huge steaks our friend Bill Rudie had packed in. Bill, a long time canoeing buddy and Terry Teich, a teacher who works with Mary Jo, came through today, meeting us on the Horse Portage just as we were completing a latrine installation. They had paddled in to join us on the trip back to town and would stay with us until then.

I wasn't complaining. After a summer of eating mostly noodles and rice, the steaks were very welcome. I watched them sizzle in the pan and stirred the potatoes frying next to them. Mary Jo was making a salad.

Yes, a salad! Not only had Bill and Terry come to our wilderness home for a visit, but my friend Sam Cook, a writer for our hometown newspaper, had come in solo to interview us. As is the way with those who have known the self inflicted deprivation of dried wilderness foods, Sam too had been thoughtful and had brought the potatoes and lettuce.

The little cabin was abuzz with conversation and laughter. It had been a long time since we had had the chance to visit with friends and though we talked with someone nearly every day, it was a great relief to relax with familiar company. Of course, when they bring their own dinner (and yours) they insure a warm welcome. I do not put a price on friendship but I would say that thick steaks and fresh lettuce, at least on a canoe trip, comes pretty near the figure.

Tomorrow we will pay them back. So very generous are we that we will let them help us dig a latrine. Though the steaks, potatoes and salad, as well as the companionship, were much appreciated, I would have traded them all for a chance to stay at Lower Basswood Falls awhile longer. There is little that the world outside, with its noise and confusion, had that could compare with what we had found here and I felt strongly that I had just begun to understand how important was that sense of oneness that came with living in the wilderness. In June the excitement of the new job had shadowed that sense, and well into July it had been submerged beneath the anger and frustration that came with dealing with some of the inconsiderate boors that had marred the beauty and silence of our part of the canoe country.

As I listened to the banter of our friends I was at once both happy and sad. Meeting friends in the bush is always cause for celebration and I was glad that they had come, was anxious to show them the glorious canoe country that had become as home to us.

And therein lay the problem. It had become home. We had become engulfed by its rhythms and moods and they had become ours. We had not so much changed the wilderness as it had changed us and we had slipped into a oneness with the land. It was important, I decided, to take that feeling of oneness with us when we left. If we could, our departure, though heavy-hearted, would be the beginning of a new challenge.

The steaks and potatoes were done. The salad was tossed. I sat down to the repast with our companions, all of us crowded around the little table in the cabin, feeling confident that when the time came, more than just memories would accompany us back to the world outside.

Started out today to replace the broken firegrate at Crooked Lake site #33. We found the site occupied and decided not to disturb the party camped there. Took the opportunity to show our friends around the area that has become so dear to us, including the pictographs, Smallmouth Rapids and a special little island.

This evening we sat in our canoes, side by side, and watched as the moon rose spectacularly through the notch that is the Canadian half of the falls. It was enormous and the color of yellow cheese and the river turned to quicksilver in its light.

◆ OLSON'S ISLAND ◆

I didn't tell anyone about it, not even Mary Jo. I have, for a long time, played a game. Whenever I read the writings of Sigurd Olson and he describes some secret route or treasured place, I would try to piece together just where that route or place might be. Today I stood on one, and shamefully kept the secret to myself.

We had planned on replacing a broken firegrate today. The very grate that had taken a short trip into the Quetico, and which we had so meticulously installed and leveled, we discovered recently had been broken. How someone had done it I'm not sure, but four of the iron rungs were missing and I would guess that after they had become red hot, a bucket of cold water thrown on them had caused them to snap. When we arrived at the site today with a replacement grate we found a party cooking breakfast and decided the job would have to wait, not wanting to disturb their trip.

A holiday ensued. We had pressed our friends into helping us dig a latrine yesterday and thought they might get some kind of a weird thrill out of installing a grate. When those plans fell through none of

us were disappointed and Mary Jo and I decided to give them the three dollar tour.

The day was hot, the blue sky speckled with pale, plump clouds. A light breeze blew warm from the northwest. The air reeked of sleep, not the weariness of great exertion, but of the leisure the north country knows only briefly in the summer. A great drowsiness drove us to shore and lunch after our tour and we landed on a small island north of the pictographs.

I had wondered about this island all summer, paddling by the forested west shore as well as the precipitous east. An apostrophe in the middle of the channel, it punctuated the entrance to Moose Bay. What I had wondered about was whether or not this island of Olson's writings was yet possessed of the magic he had described.

The packs were carried up the rock slope to an open shelf on the south end of the island. We all sat and spread out the wealth of cheese, sausage and crackers, the green lichen encrusted rock our dining table. A few large black ants came out to join us, making sure that no crumb would go to waste. There was not much said. The sun and warm breeze lulled everyone's senses and soon the silence was interrupted only by the soft snoring of nappers. I lay back on the warm rock and let the sun caress my face, finally pulling my hat down over my eyes to keep the light out and the sleep in.

I was startled awake by the gargling call of a raven. Prying my hat from my brow I looked around. Everyone was napping or merely contemplating except Sam, who had disappeared. I got up.

There is a steep hill on the center of this island and Gypsy and I walked to the top through a fine stand of pine. There was almost no sound but that of our nearly silent footsteps on the thick pine needle duff. Not a single chickadee sang in the waxy needled pines nor even a whiskey jack throwing his voice. The pines exhaled sweet scented vapors in the sun, their pitch flowing freely in their loose limbed stretch for the sky. Even the trees of the north country revel in the heat of the short summers. Reaching the crest the east side opened dramatically to me and I caught the breathtaking vista of Moose Bay to the north, miles of primary colors, blue and green mostly, in a path of

223

seduction, enticing the explorer in me to follow them deeper into the wilderness. From atop this high cliff I could look down and see how the clear waters of this bay mingled with the darker waters of Crooked and I scanned the black forest of the Canadian shore across the channel.

Sam stood on the far end of the cliff, camera in hand, shooting photos. I sat down on the warm rock and thought of what I had read.

Olson had described this island in *Open Horizons* as one of his special places of deep silence. It was "a camp on a small island above the Pictured Rocks of Crooked Lake, a rocky glaciated point looking toward the north, a high cliff on one side balanced by a mass of dark timber on the other."

What he had found here is what many people seek in the wilderness. He had found in the awesome peace of this place "a deep awareness of ancient rhythms and the attunement men seek but seldom find."

Over the course of the summer I had felt as though by merit of the crowds and problems we had dealt with that we may never find the wilderness of which Olson spoke. I had begun to question if it even existed still, that perhaps we have managed to preserve the landscape only but not the wilderness, that we had been left with a hollow shell and without the essence. If there be no stillness, there can be no wilderness.

This island, this place where Olson had said "any sound would have been a sacrilege", was the same island we had been floating near when the roar of illegal motor traffic had shattered the peace. The motors had come through at least three times since then and those who drove them had always gotten away with their deed. Would Olson have been as mad as I? I guessed we would have felt the same sadness.

But we had found the solitude of wilderness in places this summer, although it had not always been easy to find. Still, there were many more times of peace than there was of noise and the snatches of solitude we had found had worked deep into my soul. Even as I sat on that high cliff and soaked in both the sun and vistas, the quiet was complete. It had healed since severed by the passing motors. Quiet, which is the essence of wilderness, is illusionary, is prone to dissolving.

Immensely tough in fiber, wilderness is fragile in spirit and its essence can be destroyed in a moment, as it had been for hundreds of people when the roar of outboards had passed them by, as it had for those of Olson's generation when the canoe country was filled with the clamor of float planes. And, I was beginning to understand, it can be destroyed simply by the presence of too many people, too large of groups, and the noise and confusion that is inherent in crowds.

For the moment though, this was Olson's wilderness, quiet and unperturbed. I thought how sad it was then that I had never met before he died the man that was such an important part of preserving the canoe country. He would be happy to know that the places he loved and the silence he cherished are still intact, at least in some locations and at some times. The wilderness that I had sought had been here the whole time, waiting for a quiet moment to come forth, waiting for me to become receptive.

Sam walked past me as I sat musing, heading back down to the canoes, hardly uttering a word. "No one spoke." Olson had said of the spell of this place and their fear of disturbing it.

It was good to know that the spell was still here and that there were people who could still sense it. I took one last look around from the top of Olson's island and then followed Sam down the hill.

Terrific thunderstorm and driving rains passed through last night, leaving a steady, morning rain and stubborn mists well into the day. Saw Sam off this morning.

Lightning struck a large white pine on a small island just below the Canadian portage at the falls. Discovered the burning tree this morning while making my rounds in the rain. Spent most of the morning extinguishing the fire which was primarily in the trunk of the large tree. Total time elapsed: 2+ hours.

Packed in preparation for our departure.

• THANKFUL •

Gypsy and I wandered across the ridge between the cabin and the boathouse, weaving our way around patches of sodden caribou moss, leaving Mary Jo with our guests. The blueberries we had found there earlier in the summer were gone now and some of the plants had taken on a tinge of yellow and red, rushing the autumn colors.

I was not in a hurry. This would be our last evening at the cabin and now that our departure loomed so near I could scarcely believe that the summer had fled. I was feeling the need to look at everything one more time; the ridge, the boathouse, our little dock, even the rock down on the shore where I had stood so many times to fill our water bucket. Not only did I want to see everything once more, I wanted to see it with leisure, as if by paying attention to every detail I might better burn their images into my memory.

The dock at the boathouse was high and dry, a perfect place to sit. One might think that all docks were always high and dry. Not this one. When we had first arrived it was at least two feet underwater and didn't appear until sometime in July. Even then it took a week of sunny weather before the timbers were dry enough to walk on.

Wet and scummy at first, the dock was more dangerous than useful. At least a couple of times it had disappeared beneath the stained waters after heavy rainfalls. I have never seen a place such as this, the water levels fluctuating wildly even after a moderate rain.

Running parallel to shore instead of at a right angle, the dock also marked our swimming hole. The waters seemed to rarely get warm enough for a truly comfortable swim, but a dip here was always refreshing, to say the least. It was a compromise, Mary Jo had said. When the water was warm enough for a comfortable dip, it was tepid for drinking. With the boathouse nearby, we also bathed here, swimming to get wet and then hiding behind the building to strip and scrub, rinsing with buckets of water hauled from the lake. By doing so the soap fell with relatively little harm on the soil, to be broken down quickly by the microbes, and when most of the soap was swept from our skin, we would plunge back into the lake for a final swim.

Gypsy hunted frogs in the shallows. She had terrorized the frogs the entire summer, splashing after them like a racoon. I don't believe she ever caught one but the frogs entertained her mightily. I don't suppose they thought it was much fun.

I looked around for my loon. From the very beginning we had a loon who frequented this bay. I had discovered that if Gypsy and I sat quietly on the dock and I did my best loon imitation, he would converse with me. Judging by how easy he was to talk to, how quickly he responded to my calling and the fact we never saw him with another loon, I guessed he was an immature male, lonely without a mate. Many an evening I would call and he would answer my loon talk, swimming up to within feet of the dock. Gypsy always watched this with great curiosity but never once launched herself after the loon. I think she recalled how futile chasing loons is after being led far out into Tuscarora Lake when she was just a year old, the loon ever surfacing just in front of her, tempting her on. The chase lasted a half a mile before Gypsy caught on to the game.

The bay was calm. The first bats of the evening were skimming low, feeding on hatching insects. The night sounds were deadened, hollow. It had rained much today and the forest absorbed not only the moisture but any attempt at noise.

The rain had begun sometime during the night and I recalled come morning that a terrific crash of thunder had shaken me awake at one point. The morning was cloaked in mist, pouring off the falls like steam from a kettle, the lake waters starting the cooling process that would lead to ice in just a couple of months. Though it is summer by definition, the north country begins its winter countdown without consulting a calendar. For a week now the nights had been cool enough to raise mists and the mornings had been damp with dew.

The mists were gone today, washed away by the steady rain. In what Sam once called "a real frog-strangler" downpour, we stood and watched as he paddled off in his little solo canoe. Done with his story and visit he was heading home, going via the Horse River and eventually out at Mudro Lake. I had tried to sneak some of my heavier items into his pack just before he left, hoping he wouldn't discover them until well underway, thereby saving us from lugging out a few extra pounds. I must have had a goofy grin on my face as I helped him carry his gear to the dock because he stopped me short with "OK Furtman, what gives?" and dug into his pack. Seems someone had once loaded his Duluth pack with a well wrapped, but very heavy, rock which Sam didn't discover until he had unpacked at home. It wasn't likely then that he'd fall for a similar trick. And he didn't.

Walking the dog this morning after Sam had left, surveying the storm's damage, I spotted a fire on the small island below the falls, just offshore the Canadian portage. My first thought was that it must be a campfire built against the base of the tree.

It was at that point I recalled the thunder and lightning of the night before and looked further up the tree's trunk. I could see the slash of the lightning's path down the tree's length.

Hustling back to the cabin and retrieving an axe and every bucket we had, Mary Jo and I paddled to the island. Stepping up to the tree I felt its trunk. It was hot. Smoke poured out of knot holes twenty feet up, and out the spouts of hollow, broken branches. The tree was a chimney with the fire almost entirely inside, the only flames visible being the ones at the base I had mistaken for a campfire. A rent had been ripped in the trunk, three or four feet long, right up the center of the tree at about chest height. The old white pine was thick through its middle, bigger around than one could get his arms about, and leaned precariously toward the west, out over the river. I could see fire through this gash.

We quickly extinguished the flames at the base and then began pouring water into the gash. Tossing a bucket of water toward this target only resulted in most of it bouncing off the trunk, missing the three inch wide cavity. I took our axe and began chopping the hole wider, hot, steaming wood flying everywhere.

Shortly our friend Bill arrived and spelled me with the axe and Mary Jo and I served as the water brigade. With gloved hands we would reach inside the hot tree and pull long lumber-like chunks of blackened wood out the hole and toss them hissing into the river. By this time it was more steam than smoke that shot out the knotholes up the trunk. We were winning the battle. At one point I felt along the roots and discovered that they too were burning inside though there was no evidence other than the heat. Cracking one open with the axe I found that like the main trunk, it had also been completely hollowed by fire.

After two hours of chopping and tossing water the fire was out. I couldn't know if this tree would survive, but at least we had stopped it from spreading to others.

At dusk on the dock, I yodeled my best loon call but there was no reply, the call falling hushed on the waters. Someone was walking down the boathouse trail and I turned at the sound. It was Mary Jo. She walked out onto the dock and I reached up and took her hand. Without a word she sat down next to me. The falls droned sadly in the background.

"You don't want to go home, do you?" she asked.

I shook my head. No, I didn't want to leave. The thought of going back to town had weighed heavily on me for some time. I felt as though our work here was not completed. "Drive a nail home and clinch it so faithfully that you can wake up in the night and think of your work with satisfaction," the sage of Walden pond had written. I hoped we would be able to sleep soundly when we dreamed of our work here.

I was sad, too, at leaving this simple lifestyle. Thoughts of being indoors all day, of not feeling the wind in my face, the splashing of cool waters on my hand as I paddled, the thought of hanging our canoe in the garage for the long winter were not pleasant. Although I knew that it was not realistic in these modern times, I also knew that we had somehow gotten very near to how people were supposed to live and I longed not to leave it. At least, I prayed, we might be able to retain some of the simplicity and apply it to our lives on return to town.

Mary Jo put her arm around me. The sky was purple and orange, the last sunset we would see from this dock clearing the evening air of the day's moisture. The heavy dampness had lifted and the night stood before us clear. The air grew chill. Gypsy came and sat by my other side.

Mary Jo's head was on my right shoulder and I could feel the dampness of her quiet tears. She didn't want to leave, either. I lifted her face in my hands.

"We'll come back someday, Hon." I said, my own eyes brimming. "You'll see, we'll come back."

The darkness found us. It found us sitting quietly, clutching each other, sad to be leaving, thankful we had come.

*Left the cabin and boathouse for the last time and paddled
to a campsite in the south end of Friday Bay.*

*There was a slightly overcast sky with a cool, but light, breeze
from the west as we traveled the maze of Crooked saying good-
bye silently to many special spots.*

*After setting up camp, Mary Jo, Gypsy and I left Bill and
Terry for a last chance to fish this beautiful lake. We coerced a
couple of fine smallmouth into coming back to camp for dinner.
They made a delightful, and fitting, meal to end our stay in the
wilderness.*

• A SEASON FOR WILDERNESS •

They came at dusk. Perhaps a dozen of them together, the gloom
was split by a flash of black and white, the air stirred by the rapid
beating of wings, the calm gasping as the ducks swung into the south
end of Friday Bay. The ringnecks turned tightly in the narrow end of
the bay, dipped below the black pinnacled forest and headed north
past our camp. One last time I saw them as they twisted in flight and
climbed above the trees, a tight formation outlined against the fading
west sky. Then, brazen chested they let the air slip through their wings
and tumbled out of sight, dropping black against the dark forest, down
to the waiting lake. Seconds later I heard the hiss of water on their
feet and feathers as they skid to a stop.

The four of us had turned to the sound and the dog, always at my
side, tensed in tight attention. Not food, not warmth, not rest was
more important to her than ducks on the wing and she let out a small
anxious whine as they passed.

We had paddled this day to Friday Bay, leaving the cabin as empty
as when we had first arrived. My last recollection of our little wil-

derness home is a slightly watery one for I saw everything through misty eyes. I knew that in leaving that place that we were also leaving behind a part of us, leaving behind a lifestyle so simple and comfortable that it fit like an old pair of shoes. There would be future trips to the wilderness, that is sure, but I felt in my heart that life would never again be so uncomplicated as to allow us the luxury of spending three months there. We would make a point of visiting the cabin again, but the reality was that we would just be visiting, like everyone else who had stumbled across it in the woods.

Still, there was joy in the parting too, happiness in the company of our friends Bill and Terry. As Mary Jo busied herself with our departure I watched her and felt a great warmth, lucky to have been able to spend time in the wilderness with such a strong woman. Never once did her enthusiasm wane and through her adventuresome spirit I felt my own appreciation for the wilds enhanced, her excitement when seeing something new or beautiful adding to my own, her insights clarifying mine.

Though we felt saddened at having to leave what we had truly come to feel was "our territory", we left with the satisfaction of knowing we had done our best, had left the wilderness in better shape than when we had come. We had toiled to erase the signs of other's abuse, had cleaned and scrubbed, had cleared portages and dug latrines. More importantly, we felt that we had reached some of the visitors, had taught them something about caring for the wilderness and left them with the skills they needed to pass through without leaving any sign. This was a legacy we hoped would justify our frustrations and would multiply as some of them passed on to still others what we had passed to them.

We also had our animal senses awakened, how it was to feel pleasantly weary with work, our muscles harden with labor. We knew what it was like to paddle as most people walk or breathe; rhythmically, easily and without thought. The longest portages had grown short, the heaviest loads light.

In this discovery of the animal self, in the simplicity of life here, we had also come a long way toward improving our spiritual self.

Hard work at simple tasks had freed our minds of the stresses known by most people, allowing us the leisure to contemplate. We had not lacked for music or entertainment; conversation, writing and reading occupying free time to the cadence of wilderness melodies.

I had wanted to touch the pulse of the wilderness and when I had, I found it beat slowly. I also found that this pulse could in no way ever be changed, could never be sped up to match the frantic pace of a modern human, but instead, given time, would engulf the racing human pulse and smother it, forcing it to slow until finally and inevitably the two would beat in unison as they had for millenia. Whenever this unison is broken, all things become discordant, leading to unhappiness.

I had time to contemplate wilderness, bent over a shovel digging latrine holes or clutching an unbent fishing rod, and its importance.

The wilderness is the white blood cell of the body earth, staving off impurities, fighting the ills of the land. The blood count of this planet is mighty low, nearly terminally so and gets weaker by the day. It is not enough to save bits and pieces of wilderness. You can not have a healthy canoe country and ill urban centers and expect the planet to feel well. We can preserve every last tree in the canoe country, and all the trees in all the other official wilderness areas and still be doomed if we do not check the spread of cities, the suburban sprawl that eats away daily at the wild areas that have not received lawful protection. We must, each one of us, find those meadows and marshes, woodlots and creeks near our homes and deal with them with the same respect we reserve for renowned wildernesses. If we do not, the planet will simply cease to function.

Some would say that I overreacted when dealing with some of the less pleasant events we encountered this summer. Why so much wrath over a few dishes washed in a lake, a few dead fish scattered about?

I discovered that my wrath was not so much over those single instances but what they represented. The wilderness is a microcosm. It is a testing ground for attitudes and ethics.

If a man will pollute Crooked Lake without thought, what choices will he make when deciding the disposal of his factory's wastes? While

destruction in a campsite is many times more visible because of it pristine surroundings, the excess in lifestyles outside of the wilderness is many times more serious. If people do not develop a land ethic while in the wilderness, I shudder to think of the repercussions of their actions outside where the opportunity for greater destruction is manifold.

It is not so much that the solutions to the world's environmental ills are so difficult as are the choices made in approaching those solutions. The choices have to do with our lifestyles, of choosing what is best for our natural resources over what is best for our wallet and learning to control our population.

We have chosen, for the most part, to ignore the difficult choices in exchange for the merely expedient. How expedient is a race that rushes toward its own doom? All creatures depend upon each other, none live in a void. Each utilizes resources to suit its own needs but all save man return something of equal value. We have not been carrying the weight of the world's creatures, but they us. The beaver may denude a hillside but its pond becomes a feeding ground for moose, a storehouse of water for plants and fish in dry times. Mankind has the same right as the beaver, but no more, to use resources. With that right to use goes the responsibility to return something of value, to add to the diversity of nature. We have ceased to do that, however, and no longer return to the soil even the nutrients of our own bodies but lock them forever in a vault of concrete and steel.

Wilderness has been touted as a spiritual salvation for an increasingly urbanized human race, that recreation is its highest value. It is said that the wild areas of the world must be saved for the pharmacological wonders they may contain, retained as storehouses of natural resources. All of this is based on the highly egotistical attitude that wild areas exist solely for the benefit of mankind.

If there had been no campers in the BWCAW this summer, there would have been no need for us as rangers. Wilderness management is a misnomer. Wilderness needs no management, can not be improved upon. It is the people that go there that need management. Man is far less important to wilderness than wilderness is to man. It is only our egotism that allows us to believe otherwise.

Meaningful changes in restoring the ecological balance of this world will only come when all people realize that they are a part of nature, not some higher form of life that can exist without it.

When, and if, that time comes, it will be a season for wilderness, a season during which the right of wilderness to exist will no longer even be questioned, that wilderness should exist for its own benefit only. In that season we will recognize that all living things deserve to exist, not based on whether or not they are good to eat or are useful to us, but because they are every bit our equal in insuring that the complex ecosystem we all live in functions well.

Like the last evening at the cabin, I pressed myself today to imprint my memory with everything around us. Mary Jo and I had headed out after making camp to catch a last fish, to follow Crooked's winding shore, to listen to the close of yet another wilderness day. It was sweeter than most, calm and quiet, and I felt as if I must burst with the pleasure of it all. What I had taken from the wilderness could not be seen, could not be touched or smelled or tasted. But it satiated me nonetheless.

It was dark. Bill, Terry and Mary Jo had wandered over to the snapping campfire and their faces glowed gold in its light, each one thinking deep thoughts or nothing at all. Tomorrow we would paddle south through the maze of little lakes and winding river, stopping to do one last day's worth of ranger work at a few campsites along the way. The following day would find us at a landing, waiting for the USFS truck to pick us up and then a drive to our home in Duluth. It would end as it began, with no fanfare, no one but us changed and even us unsure exactly how much or in what manner. Behind us the brooding wilderness would go on much as it always had.

I stood in the darkness and listened to the ducks feeding in the bay, small guttural chuckles of happiness as they ate. When we had come to the canoe country the ducks were in pairs, the trees in new green foliage, the weather just beginning to warm. Lately the nights had begun to cool and a few yellowing birch and scarlet mountain maples had betrayed the coming of autumn. Now the ducks were flocking up, answering an ancient urge. Soon they would leave the canoe country. But they would come back in the spring, they would return to the magical north.

I found comfort in that. A cool breeze blew down the bay from the north and I clapped Gypsy to my side, turning toward the inviting comfort of the fire and my companions. Like the ducks we too would be leaving, but only for awhile.

✦COLOPHON✦

Designed by Christine Linder, Moonlit Ink, Madison, Wisconsin
Cover painting by Paul Lackner, Madison, Wisconsin
Illustrations by Susan Robinson, Grand Marais, Minnesota
Title calligraphy by Linda Hancock, Madison, Wisconsin
Type set in Sabon by Impressions, Inc., Madison, Wisconsin
Printed and bound on 55 lb. Emerson by Banta, Menasha, Wisconsin
Published by NorthWord Press Inc., Minocqua, Wisconsin